Copyright

The unauthorized reproduction or distribution of a copyrighted work is illegal. Criminal copyright infringement, including infringement without monetary gain, is investigated by the FBI and is punishable by fines and federal imprisonment.

Please purchase only authorized editions and do not participate in or encourage, the piracy of copyrighted material. Your support of author's rights is appreciated.

This book is a work of fiction. Names, characters, places and incidents are the products of the author's imagination or used fictitiously. Any resemblance to actual events, locales or persons, living or dead is entirely coincidental.

Negotiation copyrighted 2021 by Delta James

Cover Design: Dar Albert

Editing: Bre Lockhart of Three Point Author Services

❀ Created with Vellum

ACKNOWLEDGMENTS

These things are so hard to write. It can't be as long as the book, but you fear leaving people out. So instead, I'll just go with the basics:

- To my father who gave me the gift of storytelling
- To Renee and Chris without whom none of what I do would be possible
- To the Girls: Goody, Katy, Emma, Roz, Ava and Skylar
- To my Critical Reader and Focus Groups, JT Farrell and all of my readers – thank you from the bottom of my heart
- To Bre Lockhart of Three Point Author Services, Editor Extraordinaire for all her hard work and putting up with my crazy schedule
- To Dar Albert of Wicked Smart Designs, the genius behind my covers who works with nothing

from me and produces the most amazing artwork, which then become my covers

NEGOTIATION

MASTERS OF THE SAVOY

DELTA JAMES

CHAPTER 1

November 9, 1888
London, England

Tired. She was exhausted. Her plan had been to pick up another pint, but she barely had money for rent, and the rent collector was due in the morning. He'd warned her if she was late or short again, she'd be evicted on the spot. Winter was coming and she had no desire to be without even the meager shelter her squalid little room provided.

A tall, posh gentleman in an expensive greatcoat and top hat looked her way. She smiled, tried to straighten her clothes and approached him, exaggerating the sway of her hips.

"Hello, lovie. Looking for company?"

He nodded.

"Don't be shy. My room's just around the corner and I won't bite."

She held out her hand and he took it, following meekly behind her. This might not be so bad. He seemed to be polite. She might be able to deal with him quickly and have a little money for food. She watched his actions in the battered, obsidian mirror as he closed the door and rushed up behind her. *Eager chap. This might be over more quickly than I thought. Best to get my money up-front.*

The sharp tip of the knife punctured her neck, and he drew the blade across her throat. She knew she was dead, but her murderer hadn't counted on his victim being able to exact her revenge from the place that existed between life and death—heaven and hell. Her spirit rose over her body, and she drifted to the mantle, resisting the magnetic pull of the veil. She watched in horror as the man slipped out of his jacket, hanging it on the nail in the wall and rolling up his sleeves.

He stood over the body—her body—and the pocket watch that had been in his vest fell out and was stopped from hitting the floor by the fob attached to his waistcoat. Her killer laid the knife down on her body, unclasped the timepiece and placed it on the mantle by the mirror. He then proceeded to mutilate and eviscerate her body, posing her in a lewd fashion.

She blew the last of her breath on the ashes that still smoldered in the fireplace and murmured the ancient curse of her ancestors, gesturing to the looking glass that would trap him forever in the place he had murdered her.

> *Ashes to Ashes*
> *Body and Soul*
> *I curse you and your evil*
> *Beyond this mortal coil*

Her killer screamed as his body shrank in on itself until no trace of his being remained—his lifeforce banished forever into the mirror. Her revenge complete, she relinquished her hold on the realm that hung between life and death and allowed herself to drift toward the light.

Present Day
London, England

Rachel Moriarty? Had Sage enlisted one of the constables' help in making a joke? Perhaps he should speak to Roark about her penchant for making jokes of people's names.

As Holmes rounded the corner and spied her sitting there, he had to admit if she was one of Sage's creations, he'd have to rethink asking Roark to scold her. Rachel Moriarty was gorgeous—she looked a bit taller than average, with light brown hair streaked with silver and highlights from the sun. He couldn't tell a great deal from where he was standing, but she appeared to have a curvaceous figure hiding beneath her frumpy clothes.

Idly, Holmes wondered what she'd look like in a corset and G-string at Baker Street, the BDSM club he'd been frequenting. Given that Sage had created him as a foil for her fictional and now real-life hero, Roark Samuels, his penchant for dominance in sexual matters was no surprise. The club afforded him a safe, controlled way to meet his own needs, and help submissives with theirs.

It was all done with a contract in place that spelled out what both parties could expect—an experienced Dom who would see to a sub's needs in exchange for having his own met. The contract made it clear that he had no interest in anything outside the club. He never played more than twice with any sub to limit the possibility of the sub being misled.

Almost-anonymous sex had seemed ideal when he'd been introduced to the club, but the more time he spent outside of Sage's books, the more he wondered what it might be like to have a real relationship with a woman, the kind of true connection Roark had found with Sage—a private intimacy they could take out into the world and not just leave behind in the bedroom or the club.

But how do I do that? Up until a short time ago, I only existed in the pages of Sage Matthews' erotic romance novels. Do I even have anything real and substantive to offer a woman?

She was sitting in the main foyer area of Scotland

Yard's headquarters. It was a light, airy space that looked more like an upscale office building than a police station. Nothing immediately inside the doors indicated you were walking into the head office of one of the world's most revered police forces.

When Constable Landry had called up to let him know there was a woman seeking his assistance, he hadn't failed to notice the sense of humor in sending a person named Moriarty to speak with him. After all, in Sir Arthur Conan Doyle's stories of the fictional consulting detective, Holmes and Moriarty had been bitter adversaries.

"Ms. Moriarty? I'm DSI Michael Holmes. The constable seemed to think you were in some distress and that I might be able to help."

"Actually…"

So, she was American.

"It's Dr. Moriarty. And did you say Holmes?"

Holmes chuckled. "Yes, a rather unfortunate name for a detective…"

She picked up the large purse that had been sitting beside her. "And people think the English have no sense of humor. I hope your constable is having a good laugh…"

Holmes reached out to grasp her elbow lightly. "I rather suspect Landry handed you off to me because of the names. You have to admit, there's a bit of humor asking Detective Holmes to speak to Dr. Moriarty. But I can assure you I am a DSI and if you have a problem, I really would like to help. If it will make you feel any better, you can call me Michael… and I can call you…"

"Rachel," she said, glancing around speculatively. She seemed to consider his words and then nodded. "I promise you, Detective Holmes, this is not a joke on my part."

"How long have you been visiting us here in England?"

"What makes you think I'm not a citizen?" she challenged, bringing her chin up a notch.

So, the girl had spirit—dreadful taste in clothing—but she was feisty. The first would be welcome and the second he could fix.

She shook her head. "The accent. It was my accent. You're a detective; of course, you would have figured that out. My apologies, DSI Holmes. It seems my nerves are getting the better of me and I'm lashing out."

He chuckled. "I thought you were going to call me Michael? Let me assure you, Rachel, if that is your idea of lashing out, you and I should get along famously. Why don't we get out of the lobby?"

Holmes escorted her down a short hall and into a private interview room. As he held out a chair, he noticed how she sank into it like a dancer might, beautifully and gracefully. *Would she be able to sink to her knees that elegantly?* Visions of a naked Rachel Moriarty, on her knees in a classic submissive's pose, presenting herself to him as her Dom flashed through his mind and made his cock come to attention in a way it never had before.

God, I really need to find the time to get to Baker Street. The problem is that having met Rachel Moriarty, I don't know that I want to play with anyone else—and I'm not sure that playing is what I want to settle for.

He took a seat across from her and tried to banish from his mind the image of her naked and waiting for his pleasure. With the table providing cover, at least she wouldn't be able to see the way his cock was tenting his wool trousers. "Now, what brings you to Scotland Yard?"

"I don't think this is a good idea."

"I assure you, it is. Something concerned you enough to bring you here and walk down that hall with me, even after you thought someone was making a joke at your expense. I'd like to know what that was," he said, his voice strong and compassionate.

"You're going to think I'm crazy, but I'm not."

"Go on," he urged gently, but firmly.

She breathed in deeply and nodded. She was nervous—no not nervous per se—but agitated. She folded her hands into her lap and then brought them back up to rest on the table. Even though his voice and demeanor had been gentle, Rachel Moriarty didn't seem to want to look him in the eye. If she was submissive by nature, she might readily react well to a hint of dominance in his voice. She seemed ready to respond to an authority figure telling her what to do. That could make handling her, both personally and professionally, easier.

"I hold a PhD in English History, specializing in the War of the Roses through the reign of Elizabeth I. Five years ago, I relocated to London and began my business, Select Tours. I focus on small, private tours catered to an individual or small group's specific interests."

He nodded, approvingly. "I've heard good things about your company. I have friends at the Savoy, and they speak well of you."

"You have? I mean, I work with the Savoy, and they send quite a bit of business my way. I just wouldn't think a detective with the Yard had a lot of reason to frequent one of London's most famous hotels. Your accent pegs you as born and raised in London, the West End if I'm not mistaken."

Now, she was showing off. Was she trying to impress him? That wouldn't be difficult. She was intelligent, beautiful, articulate, and unless he missed his guess, submissive. Holmes smiled. "You have an ear for accents, Rachel. I was born and raised not far from Leicester Square. A few months ago, you took a friend of mine on a tour she still raves about—Sage Matthews."

"The author?," she said, looking him in the eye for the first time and smiling. She felt more confident now that she seemed on more familiar ground.

"Lovely person. So kind and unassuming. I didn't know what to expect when I met her, but she was charming, intelligent and incredibly curious. Her husband seems quite intimidating…"

"He can be, but he's madly in love with Sage. Roark and I have been friends for years. I've never known him to be as happy and settled as he is now."

Despite their casual conversation, Rachel's body remained tense, as if she was unused to relaxing in the presence of another. Intrigued, he wondered if a session with a caring Dom—him to be specific— might be just what she needed to quiet an obviously busy mind and keen intellect. If she allowed him to, Holmes was certain he could help her find a peaceful place where she could just be.

"Yes; they did seem to have a very intimate and loving connection…" Her sentence drifted off as if her mind had disconnected from what they were talking about.

"But I don't suppose you came here to talk to me about the Savoy's most illustrious couple."

"No," she said, refocusing on him. "No, I didn't. You're going to think I'm crazy…"

"You said that before, and I told you I wouldn't. You need to start trusting that I'm not going to lie to you."

She nodded again, bringing her hands up from her lap and folding them together. "I was in Whitechapel, conducting a tour after dark. We were in the actual room where Mary Jane Kelly met her end…"

"I didn't know they allowed people in there."

She smiled. It transformed her face even though the smile did not reach her eyes. The windows to her soul remained guarded.

"I keep my tours small and intimate, and I have a doctorate in English history…"

"Jack the Ripper operated in the time of Queen Victoria, long after Elizabeth the First."

This time, Rachel's smile was genuine, lighting up her countenance. "Yes, but it fascinates people to this day, and part of the key to my success has been catering my tours to each client."

He nodded. "I'm sorry. I shouldn't have interrupted you. Please, go on."

"We were headed back to the main street when I noticed the door to her room was slightly ajar. I was certain I had locked it. As I grasped the knob to check it, I felt someone push hard on the door from the other side—someone strong. Before it slammed shut, I thought I heard a scream. Then I felt a powerful force—a gush of wind and energy—come through the door and pass through my body. It was quite unsettling."

Holmes reached across the desk, covering her hands with his own. "I can only imagine."

"To make matters worse, for the past several nights, I've awakened in my flat in Charing Cross feeling like someone was inside. The door to my balcony has been open, even though I know for certain I closed and locked it. And there's an icy chill…" Her gaze drifted, as if lost in memory. Then she snapped her attention back to him.

"This was a mistake," she said, withdrawing her hands and standing. "I'm sure you think…"

Rising with her, he spoke gently, wanting to keep her with him. Safe. "What I think, Rachel, is that something has frightened you and you're in need of help. I'm not sure that I can do anything for you officially, but I do think I should ring up Roark and have him and Sage meet us for lunch. We'll have Roark treat us to lunch at the Savoy."

"I couldn't possibly presume…"

Holmes grinned at her. "Maybe not, but I can. That's what old friends are for. Besides, he's loaded, and the Savoy has an exceptional menu."

CHAPTER 2

This was a mistake. Going to Scotland Yard had been an act of desperation, but the constable had written her off as a joke. It wasn't her fault that her last name belonged to a notorious fictional villain. And now, Detective Holmes had whisked her off to the Savoy Hotel to have lunch with a famous author. Was she even dressed for lunch at the Savoy? As she fretted, she listened to Holmes' half of the phone conversation with his friend, wishing she could just call the whole thing off.

"Roark? It's Holmes. I'm bringing Rachel Moriarty to the Savoy to have lunch with you and Sage. You're buying." *Pause.* "Yes, that Dr. Moriarty, and she didn't share the constable's sense of humor about our last names. She's had a bit of a fright and I'd like to have you talk with her."

She cut in before he could say anything else. "This

really isn't necessary, Detective Holmes. I appreciate what you're doing, but there's no need to fob me off on Mr. Samuels. I'm quite sure I can't afford his services. Besides, I must just be imagining things. I've been frightfully busy and am exhausted."

The detective gave her a quick side-glance. "All the better to let the professionals handle it. Roark owes me. I'm calling in a marker, so you won't need to worry about a bill."

"I really couldn't…"

"You really could, and you will. That's the end of it, Rachel."

Holmes escorted Rachel to his vehicle and drove them to the elegant hotel. The Savoy had opened in 1889 and was the only five star hotel on the River Thames. He pulled into valet parking and got out of the car, handing the keys over to one of the attendants. Another valet opened her door, provoking a stifled cry from her lips. While she hadn't been joking with Detective Holmes, she also hadn't shared the entire extent to which this whole experience had begun to unnerve her.

The truth wasn't that she kept waking up in the middle of the night to find the door open; it was that she sat up every night, too terrified to close her eyes, watching as the terrace door unlocked itself and slowly swung open of its own volition. The fact was, she hadn't slept for days.

Holmes was at her side in an instant, moving

quickly and quietly for such a tall, muscular man. His accent might peg him for the West End, but she felt fairly certain his suit had been custom made in the famed Savile Row. The cut was exquisite, and she couldn't imagine those broad shoulders and powerful arms and thighs would fit in something off the rack.

"Rachel are you all right?" he asked.

"Yes, umm, he just startled me."

He gave her a look that said he didn't quite believe her, but he wasn't going to pursue it—at least not at this time. She very much doubted Michael—no, she needed to think of him as DSI Holmes—missed much and let even fewer things slide. Taking hold of her upper arm with protective gentleness, he walked her into the hotel.

Five years should have been long enough to get over what had driven her here, but it wasn't. Five years, and she was still trying to get used to the fact that in the UK, cars were right-hand drive and people drove on the wrong side of the road. She'd gotten used to doing it, but it still seemed like an anomaly. There were still times she longed for a really good cheeseburger and fries. English food wasn't as bad as it was reported to be, but she had yet to find a place that served a truly good burger with all the fixings.

They entered the hotel and headed into the Savoy Grill. She'd only been here once for a business breakfast. The food had been superb, but the prices a little too high for her budget. Even so, she would have to insist on paying for her own lunch.

As they entered the restaurant, the maître d' approached, his air respectful and attentive. "DSI Holmes, Mr. Samuels called down to tell us you'd be coming. He and Mrs. Samuels will be down momentarily."

He showed them to a lovely table for four in a secluded corner that afforded them some privacy. The room was a comforting mixture of casual and elegant. Large chandeliers lit the room, but the walls were paneled in wood that seemed to have been there for centuries. The round tables were covered in cream-colored tablecloths with fine table settings, but the chairs were leather and wood. Holmes held her chair and then helped her get settled by the window, taking up the seat opposite her.

"I'm a little surprised they know you," she confessed.

Holmes gave a little shrug. "As I said, Roark and I are old friends and I'm the liaison between the Yard and the Savoy. If something comes up, I'm the one they call and vice versa. If we need something from the hotel, I pick up the phone and call Felix, who is the head concierge. It's all very friendly and informal."

"I hate feeling like I'm taking up your or Mr. Samuels' time, and I'm quite sure Ms. Matthews had better things to do."

"You'd be wrong," said Sage Matthews as she breezed in and waited for her husband to hold her chair.

"I still don't understand why it is that people don't use your proper name," said her husband, his voice low and intimidating.

Sage reached over and patted her hand. "It's nice to see you again, Rachel." Then, she turned to her husband. "As I've told you, we're going to continue to use my maiden name as my pen name because we have so much time, effort and money invested in my brand."

"I don't like it," he said, taking a seat next to DSI Holmes.

"A fact you have made abundantly clear to anyone who will listen," quipped Sage.

"If I were you, wife, I'd take some care with your behavior."

"If you were me, we'd be even kinkier than we are," Sage returned with a wicked smile.

And with that, Roark Samuels smiled—his obvious love and adoration of his wife clear in the way he looked at her.

If the intimidating Roark Samuels had spoken to Rachel in the deep, gravelly voice he'd used on his wife, she felt certain one of two things would have happened. Either she would have run like hell, or she'd have had an orgasm. Probably the former.

Although she had to admit, she enjoyed the sound of DSI Holmes' deep, dark voice even better.

As he sat listening to his friends, his gaze slid to hers. She rather imagined he could be quite seductive if he tried. Demanding too, perhaps. Appealingly so. The fact was, she was inordinately aroused by him, when he had done nothing other than be totally professional with her. *Oh dear.*

"Have you two had a chance to look at the menu?" asked Roark, distracting her from her thoughts.

"I'm going to have them make me a salad," said Sage.

"We're going to have the Beef Wellington," countered Roark.

DSI Holmes looked at her. "You'll have to forgive them, as Sage is under the mistaken impression that she is something other than gorgeous. They have this argument on a regular basis."

"You're as bad as he is," said Sage, sticking out her tongue at him.

Holmes laughed. "When are you going to get a handle on that spitfire you married?"

"Who says I want to?" Roark returned.

Rachel smiled. It was so obvious that these three people were close friends. She felt like an interloper. The truth was, she'd forgotten what it was like to have good friends. Watching the three interact now, she had to question whether she'd ever had any at all.

"I'll just have the chilled cucumber soup, and I insist on paying for my own lunch. I hadn't expected to end up here at the Savoy."

Roark rolled his eyes. "Another one. Ms. Moriarty…"

"It's Dr. Moriarty," she and Holmes said in unison.

"Dr. Moriarty, then. I would appreciate it if you would have a proper lunch, or else I shall never hear the end of it from my beloved wife. The gnocchi is excellent, as is the swordfish. And you will not be paying the bill. I live here. Trust me, you'll never see one."

"Roark is right," agreed Sage. "We just run a tab. And the gnocchi is divine."

"Would you rather have gnocchi, sweetheart?" Roark asked solicitously. "Holmes enjoys the Beef Wellington; I'm sure he'd split it with me."

"No, Roark. I'll share the Wellington with you."

Roark smiled benignly. "Such a good girl when you try."

Holmes laughed. "I'd tell you two to get a room, but then you already have one. I'll have the ribeye with chimichurri."

When the waiter arrived, Roark ordered for the entire table. Apparently Rachel was having gnocchi, which was good because it sounded exceptional, and she loved gnocchi.

Once the order was completed, Roark turned his

piercing gaze on her. "So, what has Holmes leaving his post and bringing you to my doorstep?"

Rachel's body immediately tensed. "I... I didn't ask him to leave his office and bring me to see you here at the Savoy."

"Of course not. But if he didn't think you needed my help, he wouldn't have brought you here."

"It's silly," she started, glancing around the table before looking back down. Why was she having such difficulty looking these people in the face? Was it because her story seemed so preposterous—even to her?

Holmes frowned. "No, Rachel, it isn't. She had a bit of an unsettling visit to Mary Kelly's room and ever since, she keeps waking up to find the door from her balcony has been opened."

"That must be terrifying," said Sage. "I don't know that I could sleep by myself if that was happening to me."

Rachel looked at Sage and shook her head. "I don't sleep—at least not since that visit to 13 Miller's Court."

"You didn't tell me that," said Holmes.

She turned her gaze back to Holmes. "Because I didn't want you to think I was some frightened little rabbit."

"I would never think of you that way. But if we're going to work together to get to the bottom of this, you need to tell me the truth... all of it."

"Holmes was right to bring you," Roark said firmly. "This isn't the kind of thing that the Yard is equipped to deal with."

"I'm aware of your reputation, Mr. Samuels. And I'm not sure I can afford you," Rachel said, finding it difficult to redirect her gaze to Roark.

Roark laughed. "I rather imagine Holmes is expecting me to give you the friends and family discount, which is to say, you're not to worry about the bill. Holmes, I'm sure, will be providing assistance. And he's right; you mustn't keep anything to yourself. A lie by omission is a lie all the same, and gets handled the same way, doesn't it, sweetheart?" At that last comment, he glanced pointedly at his wife, who blushed.

After recovering her composure, Sage turned to Rachel. "Why don't you tell us what happened?"

"I told DSI Holmes that I had a client who asked for a tour of the Ripper murder scenes. We were at Mary Kelly's room..." She waved a hand, embarrassed. "I feel foolish. I'm sure this is all just my overactive imagination. I'm very sorry to have bothered any of you." She stood, intending to leave before she took up any more of their time or embarrassed herself further.

"Sit down, Rachel." Holmes' voice had gone deep and taken on a commanding undertone. When she didn't move, he looked her square in the eye. "I said, sit down, Rachel."

She found herself sitting back down, unable to hold his gaze. Why was it so easy to acquiesce to his authority? The butterflies fluttering in her most feminine parts would indicate it wasn't just because he was a DSI with the Yard. The man was brutally handsome, had the most delicious voice and made her blood heat in a way it hadn't done in a very long time.

He looked at the others. "Rachel told me she saw the door to the room was still open. She was certain she had closed and locked it, but given that she had special permission to enter, she went to secure it. But it slammed shut on its own, just as she heard a scream." He paused, then turned to her. "I didn't think to ask, but did you try the door after it closed?"

"Yes. I turned the knob, and it was locked."

Holmes nodded. "She also said when it closed, she felt a powerful surge of energy pass through her body. Since then, she has been waking up in the middle of the night to see her balcony door open, even though she'd closed and locked it." He eyed her. "But as I understand it, that isn't the case. You haven't slept since the incident."

"I'm sure I'm just overtired, and my mind is imagining things."

Again, she tried to stand, but Holmes' hand covered hers, prompting her to be still. "I'm not going to tell you again. Sit down."

Before Rachel could say anything, Sage laid her hand on her arm. "You might want to do what

Michael tells you. I think you may have awakened the sleeping Dom. You're frightened, you didn't tell him everything, and you may be in danger."

"I'd listen to her if I were you," said Holmes in that rich, decadent voice of his.

She rather suspected in the right circumstances and with the right words, he could damn near talk her to orgasm. *Orgasm?* Now, where had that thought come from? DSI Holmes was having the most profound effect on her. She had to refocus on what he was actually saying versus just listening to the sound of his voice.

"Have you or have you not slept since the incident?" he continued.

"No," she whispered.

"Has anything else happened that seems out of the ordinary?" She hesitated. "Roark is right, a lie by omission is still a lie. I don't like it when you lie to me."

Biting her lip, she decided to confess what she'd held back earlier. "I keep feeling as though someone or something is following me. I'm sure I'm being paranoid, and the lack of sleep isn't helping."

Just then, the waiter approached with their meal. If the aromas coming from his direction were any indication, she was in for a treat. He set their plates in front of them, and they each began to eat. She watched as Roark expertly sliced the Beef Wellington, putting a piece on his plate before exchanging plates with Sage.

Beside her, Holmes cut into his steak, watching her. Obediently, she took a bite of the gnocchi, which practically melted in her mouth. Talk about flavor! It was almost enough—almost—to distract her from her troubles. Really, the entire meal, food and wine, were fabulous. For a moment, she gave in and just sighed in relaxation as she enjoyed the moment. Then the conversation pulled her back to reality.

"I think after we eat, we need to find Rachel a place to stay where she'll be safe and she can get some rest," said Holmes.

Roark nodded. "Agreed. We can get her a room here…"

"At the Savoy? There's no way I could afford that…"

Both men looked at her, eyebrows raised, as though she'd lost what little sense she might still have.

"I will only say this once," growled Holmes. "Under no circumstances are you to go back to your flat by yourself."

Opening her mouth to protest, Rachel caught Sage's eye. But Roark cut in before either of the ladies could speak. "And before the two of you get it into your heads that we're being overly protective or bossy, going together doesn't count."

Holmes nodded. "Either Roark or I will go with you to collect some of your things."

Rachel felt herself stiffen. "You can't tell me that I can't go home."

"I can and will—to keep you safe. You'll follow my instructions or there will be discipline—and not the fun kind. Am I clear?"

Her fear giving way to anger, Rachel set her fork firmly down on the table and stared at Holmes in defiance. "Who do you think you are?" she demanded.

Somehow, Holmes' expression got even firmer, more determined. "I'm the DSI who's running this case," he retorted, "and I will ensure your safety at all times." He inhaled deeply, then turned to his friend. "Roark, might I impose on you to keep Rachel with you while I go back to the Yard, arrange for some leave and go to Rachel's to get some of her things?"

"This is getting out of hand!" snapped Rachel.

Roark and Holmes both pinned her with a stare. Squirming, she tried and failed to think of a comeback. With a gentle sigh, Sage shook her head at the two men.

"You two are scaring poor Rachel and behaving dreadfully. Honestly, Michael I expect that kind of behavior from Roark, but usually you're far more civilized. Why don't Rachel and I go up to our room? She can borrow one of the many nightgowns that I never wear, get comfortable and see if she can't get some sleep. You two can run by the Yard and then go by Rachel's flat and have a look around. After you've seen it, we can figure out where to go from there."

"Does it ever bother you that she's far more intelligent than you?" quipped Holmes.

Roark laughed gently. "No, I'm rather used to it."

When they finished lunch, Holmes and Roark escorted the ladies upstairs. The Samuels' suite was beautiful, with a commanding view of the Thames. Rachel handed the keys to her flat to Holmes and wrote down the address.

Meanwhile, Roark smacked his wife's ass with more than just a touch of sting. "You lock the door behind us, and don't open it to anyone."

"Yes, Roark."

The two men left, and Sage dutifully threw the night latch.

"This is silly," said Rachel. "You don't need to go to all this trouble."

"It's no trouble at all. I need to do the final edits on a new book." She put a finger to her lips, studying Rachel. "Let me get you a nightgown. Don't feel weird about wearing it. I absolutely love them, but Roark won't let me wear one. So I buy them, and they hang in the closet."

"He's rather commanding—actually, both of them are."

Sage smiled at her as she handed her a beautiful silk negligee. "They're both Doms. What do you expect?"

CHAPTER 3

"What do you make of her story?" asked Roark, as they left Scotland Yard.

Holmes hesitated a moment, then gave a frustrated huff. "I don't know what happened, but I do think something happened. She's terrified. I don't know how I missed that. I'm usually far more observant."

"That would be because you're looking at her like a hungry Dom who's craving more than a snack."

"I was not…" he said, looking at Roark sharply.

"For God's sake, Holmes, I'm not criticizing. She's absolutely lovely. You're going to need to work with her about her clothes, of course—they're dreadful. Gail may have tried to kill Sage, but at least she taught her how to dress."

Holmes snorted. "I suspect those frumpy clothes

are hiding a luscious figure. And you're right; I really needed to focus on what she was saying instead of indulging my fantasies about seeing her naked."

"That's the spirit."

Holmes and Roark got to Rachel's flat in Charing Cross and let themselves in. Despite giving it a thorough examination, they found nothing amiss. Holmes paid special attention to the door to the balcony.

"Appears normal. Lock seems to be in good working order." He turned to find Roark going through her fridge.

"I figure she won't be back here so I thought I'd throw out anything that might expire." He held up a particularly ripe Chinese take-out container. "She shares our taste in food."

"I don't feel anything off in here, do you?"

"No, but that doesn't mean something strange isn't going on."

"What do you say I pack a bag for Rachel while you arrange for a room for her at the hotel?"

"I'm happy to do that, but wouldn't you prefer she be at your place?"

"I would, but if I'm going to work this case, I'd prefer she wasn't left alone."

Roark nodded. "Good thinking. I'll call and see what I can arrange. One bedroom or two?"

"Don't be an ass, Roark."

"One or two?"

"Make it a one-bedroom suite. I'll sleep on the couch."

"Of course, you will," his friend quipped.

Holmes narrowed his eyes. "Not all of us have a damsel in distress come into their lives so they can sweep her off her feet, into their bed and get a ring on their finger."

Unperturbed, Roark continued tossing out old food. "Don't tell me you can't spot your own happily ever after when it walks into Scotland Yard."

Holmes smiled. "She is rather spectacular, isn't she?"

"And she seemed to respond rather well when you quit thinking with your dick and let your Dom take over."

"She did, didn't she?" Bag packed, Holmes felt satisfied they'd done all they could at Rachel's place. On to the next part of the investigation. "What do you say we run by Mary Kelly's place and see if we can find out anything?"

Roark looked at his watch. "I have a better idea. Why don't we call it a day and get you and the lovely Dr. Moriarty set up at the Savoy?"

"I don't want her to see a bill, Roark."

"Not to worry. We can clue Felix and Gabe in. We'll keep her safe."

"We need to figure out what's going on," said Holmes.

"Indeed."

A quick call later, and Roark had arranged for Rachel to have a suite on the same floor as his and Sage's. The two men went by Holmes' place so he could pick up some things. His Victorian row home across the cobbled street from the River Thames would have been far too expensive for most other DSIs with the Yard, but Sage had written his character as having family money. Holmes smiled, thinking of the level of detail Sage had written for even her secondary characters. No wonder her readers were always asking about them and whether or not they might get their own story. Even though it was far too big for just him, Holmes loved the place. It was done in a warm, casually elegant and stereotypically English style. When they returned to the Savoy, they immediately hailed Felix Spenser, the head concierge and a trusted comrade.

"What's up?" asked Felix, the last of the trio of characters that had somehow stepped out of the pages of Sage's series of novels and had cast Roark as the primary protagonist in each story.

Unlike Roark and Holmes, he looked nothing at all like she had described: a sort of homage to Agatha Christie's Hercule Poirot—a short, round man with an egg-shaped head and cat-green eyes. The Felix who existed in this time and space was a tall man, sleek, lean, but powerfully built, with a small, vertical scar by his left eye, deep brown eyes, sensual mouth, and chestnut brown hair. In the original novels, Sage had described Roark as a muscle-bound hunk that had contrasted with the soft, round Felix. But here in the real world there was a grace and power to Felix that was only emphasized by his impeccably tailored suit.

"Let's meet with Gabe in his office," answered Holmes.

The man's eyebrow quirked up, clearly intrigued. He turned to the desk clerk, one of the hotel's senior employees, whose short silver hair was cut in the latest style. "Jenny, let Gabe know we're waiting for him in his office. And could you cover my desk for me?"

"Absolutely," she said.

They went into Gabe's office and waited; he joined them in short order.

The head of the Savoy's security team, Gabriel Watson was the only one of the four friends who hadn't once been a character in Sage's books. And he remained unaware of how Felix, Roark and Holmes had come into being.

A little less than a year ago, all three men had been characters in Sage's series of books about a mythical detective/gun-for-hire. Felix and Holmes had found themselves in the real world shortly before Roark had broken through in the nick-of-time to save Sage's life from an assassin, hired by her former publisher. Gabe had already been in the real world and had acted as if the three of them had always been there. He had become a good friend, and

Holmes sometimes regretted that they weren't always completely honest with him.

"Gentlemen?" Gabe said by way of greeting as he walked in.

Watson was a tall man, heavily muscled with the air of someone who could handle himself and any situation that came at him. His shortish blond hair had been slicked back and his icy blue eyes, which somehow managed to still seem warm, were set in a face that seemed sculpted from stone swept the room, assessing the situation.

"You have a new guest, Rachel Moriarty…"

"Moriarty?" Gabe chuckled. "Seriously? So we have Holmes, Watson, Adler and Moriarty? All we need now is a good mystery."

Corinne Adler, whose long, blonde hair was usually up in either a messy bun or held back in a cascading ponytail of sunshine and summer, was the night concierge at the Savoy, and Felix's trusted assistant. She, like Watson, was also not a character from Sage's books.

"We may have one," said Holmes, smiling as he thought about how seamlessly they had all fit into the reality in which the three of them—Roark, Felix and himself—now found themselves. Gabe had become a trusted friend, although it continued to nag at Holmes that Watson, like the rest of the world, had no idea of their true origins. "Rachel came to the Yard this morning. One of the constables gave her to me, thinking it was funny. Something weird is going on, so we moved her out of her flat. Roark got us a suite on their floor, where she can be safer. We'll be staying here until we figure this out."

Gabe groaned, as he sank into his comfortable desk chair. "Please don't tell me she has a publisher ripping her off and trying to kill her."

Roark, Felix and he had only come into being when Sage's former publisher had tried to have Sage murdered to cover up her embezzlement scheme. When they had come through the veil, everyone around them seemed to believe they had always been there. As far as Gabe was concerned, the four of them —Gabe, Roark, Felix and Holmes—had known each other for years.

"I'm afraid not. This is weirder and spookier. Every night her balcony door gets opened and there's nobody there," said Holmes.

"I think I like the hired killer better," said Gabe, with a wry grin. One of the interesting things about Watson was that while he took his job and the hotel's security seriously, he seemed to take the rest of life with a kind of sardonic humor. "What is it about you, Roark, that attracts these crazies?"

Holmes bristled. "She's not crazy, Gabe. She's scared, and we're going to help her," he growled.

Gabe shook his head, running his hands through his blond mane. "Aww, shit. Holmes, how can you do this to me? I was counting on you. You've really let me down."

"How so?"

Gabe grinned. "Roark and I had a bet. He said you'd be the next to fall; I bet on Felix."

"You did?" asked Felix, in a somewhat astonished tone. "That's rather nice of you, Gabriel."

"I haven't fallen for anybody," argued Holmes.

Gabe laughed out loud. "You just keep telling yourself that, buddy boy. Oh well, more subs for me at Baker Street. Oh, shit, is she a sub?"

Holmes shook his head, scowling at Watson who was grinning like the Cheshire Cat. "I only just met her this morning. I don't know if she's a sub, but I do know she's submissive."

"Not to worry. Just let me know when you're both going to be out of the hotel, and I'll keep an eye on her. What do you want me to do if she decides to leave?"

"Why would she do that?"

Gabe rolled his eyes that were still sparkling with amusement. "Don't you read Sage's books? The heroine always tries to leave the protection of the hero. That way the hero—that would be you, by the way—has a reason to spank her pretty ass and then make wild, passionate love to her. Who knew that women love this kind of thing? And why the hell can't one of them fall into my lap?"

Rachel woke disoriented, but not afraid—a rare respite. Up until now, she'd caught a fitful nap here and there, but as soon as the sun went down, the fear crept down her spine, ensuring she'd spend another night watching the clock, waiting for the lock to twist and the door to open. Here at the Savoy, she felt safe. Perhaps it wasn't surprising, then, that this was the first time in days that she'd had any significant sleep.

"Oh, you're awake," said Sage as she came in from the sitting room to check on her.

Sage and her husband were permanent residents at the Savoy and had one of the gorgeous, Edwardian one-bedroom suites with a commanding view of the River Thames. It boasted a spacious, by hotel standards, marble foyer and cloakroom area which led into the suite's separate sitting area and bedroom. The en-suite bath was decorated with the Savoy's trademark black and white checkerboard floor and featured a claw-foot tub and separate shower.

The room had been given a mini-makeover to more closely align with its residents' taste and to allow for a desk with dual monitors and an ergonomic chair for Sage to work at. There was also a white board hung over the desk where various story ideas and plot points were noted.

Rachel sat up, gently rolling her neck and shoulders, trying to wake up. "I really didn't think I'd go out like that."

"I'm not surprised. You looked exhausted and, for lack of a better word, haunted. How many days have you not slept?"

"A little over a week. I can catnap during the day, but at night, I'm afraid to even close my eyes. I probably should have found a cheap motel instead of staying at my apartment." She glanced at the clock, noting that several hours had passed. "Obviously I needed the sleep."

"Why don't you come into the sitting room? With my Keurig, I can make you a proper cup of coffee."

Rachel smiled. "I think I might like that even more than the nap. I keep trying to make myself learn to like tea, but I'm afraid it's a losing proposition."

"Yes, if giving up my coffee in favor of tea is a prerequisite for citizenship, I'm afraid Roark is going to have to give up on that idea."

"When did you move here? Were you and Roark married at the time? I'm sorry, that's none of my business."

"Don't worry about it. It's a unique story, one I don't mind sharing. I came over last year for an author signing, almost got murdered, met Roark and fell madly in love. Thus, I never went home." Sage smiled. "We're going to go to North Carolina later this year so I can dispose of my things. Some I'll probably ship and put into storage until we decide what we really want to do—where we want to live."

Rachel held up a hand. "Wait. Someone tried to kill you?"

Sage nodded. "Yes, my ex-publisher was embezzling from me and was afraid she would be found out. So, she ordered an assassin to seduce me at a local pub. He tried to garrote me under one of the bridges along the river—it gave me nightmares for months."

"I don't doubt you'd have nightmares."

"Honestly, they didn't start until I was investigating the Ripper murders." Sage made Rachel a cup of coffee. "By the way, I just heard from Roark. He and Michael are on their way back and are going to pick up some curry for us. If you don't like Indian food, they can get something else."

"No, that's fine, but I really don't want to be any trouble. I guess the lack of sleep was really getting to me. I don't know what I was thinking going to Scotland Yard."

"I think something frightened you at the site of the last Jack the Ripper murder. Grisly business. I did some research once about it. I had this idea for a steampunk romantic mystery set during the Fall of Terror…"

"Autumn of Terror," corrected Rachel automatically. "Sorry, bad habit."

"No problem. Anyway, after the third night of Roark having to wake me from terrifying dreams, he put his foot down and that was the end of that. It was really horrendous."

Rachel nodded. "It was. What must have been the most terrifying thing was that he was never caught. Can you imagine being a woman living in the East End at the time? Looking over your shoulder, wondering if someone walking on the street beside you might be him?"

"I know. I kept having nightmares of being chased under one of the bridges that cross the Thames and being killed—only in my dreams I was awake while he was carving me up." Sage shuddered. "Thus, the reason Roark decreed that project to be dead. He much prefers my kinkier romances, except for the menage and reverse harem. He scotched those ideas before they ever got off the ground. Did I just say 'thus' again? I really do wish they had an app I could run my spoken words through to look for repeats."

"They're your books! How can he just decide you can't write them?"

Sage laughed. "I can't decide if you're just too polite or not very observant."

"What do you mean?" Rachel asked.

Just then, Roark popped his head into the room, waving a bag of take-out food in their direction. The sharp scent of spicy Indian food wafted through the air, reminding Rachel that she was, in fact, rather hungry.

"What my sweet wife is trying to tell you," said

Roark, "is that we have a D/s relationship and while I can be a very indulgent Dom, at the end of the day she leaves most of the decision-making to me."

"I don't think I could ever do that," said Rachel.

"You'd be surprised," said Holmes. Behind him walked another strikingly beautiful man, younger than she normally found attractive, but she could certainly see the allure he would have for some. Allure? Who was she kidding? She was fairly sure that the young man's Viking god looks left younger women falling at his feet.

"You look beautiful, Rachel," Holmes added, bringing her attention back to him. Then to his words.

She glanced down and realized she was sitting in a hotel room, dressed only in a nearly transparent nightgown, with three gorgeous men staring at her. She wasn't sure whether she should run to the bedroom and get dressed or find another way to cover up. Rachel opted to grab the soft, cashmere throw that was strewn across the back of the couch and cover herself as best she could.

"I hope you like curry," Holmes continued. "We weren't sure if you'd be awake, so we brought something that we could re-heat later. By the way, this is Gabriel Watson." He pointed at the young man, who gave her a polite nod. "He's the head of security here at the Savoy. I know—Holmes, Watson and Moriarty.

It gets worse. The night concierge's name is Corinne —wait for it—Adler."

In spite of herself, Rachel laughed. "You're kidding, right?"

Holmes held up his hand. "My hand to God."

Gabe started to walk toward her, as if to shake her hand, but a low growl from Holmes stopped him in his tracks.

"I'd better get dressed. I'll need to get a cab," she said.

"A cab? Where do you think you're going?" asked Holmes.

"As much as I appreciate the lunch and the nap, I do need to get home."

"We settled this at lunch. The Savoy has a nice suite on this floor. I went to your place and packed a bag for you, then went by my place to get what I would need for a few days. I put our things in the room."

"You can't just decide to move me out of my flat and into a shared room with you."

"I think you'll find that I can and did. Rachel, there is absolutely nothing wrong with the lock on your balcony door. I believe you when you say that you keep waking up to find it open, and I don't believe for a minute that somehow you didn't lock it or some kind of natural phenomenon opened it. Something is going on…"

"Something that's kept her from sleeping at night for at least a week," supplied Sage.

Holmes glanced at Sage before glaring at Rachel. He put the curry on the table and took hold of her arm. "The rest of you should eat. If you'll excuse us, Rachel and I need to have a little discussion about the withholding of vital information."

CHAPTER 4

Rachel couldn't believe that he didn't wait for her to respond or even to see if she was opposed to his idea. He simply took hold of her arm and marched her out the door. By the time she could even think how to respond, she'd been escorted down the hall, ushered into the suite they were apparently sharing, and Holmes had closed and locked the door behind them.

Wrenching her arm from his grasp, Rachel turned on him. "Just who do you think you are, Detective Holmes?" she said, adopting a more aggressive posture—her hands clenched into fists at her side.

Holmes didn't back away; instead, he stepped into her space. "I'm a Detective Superintendent with Scotland Yard. I am not some wet-behind-the-ears schoolboy. You do not leave out pertinent information, such as you haven't slept at night since you conducted that tour of Mary Kelly's room. That's something I should have found out from you, not Sage. What the hell else aren't you telling me?"

Rachel took a step back, re-establishing her personal space and crossed her arms over her chest. "How dare you yell at me! For your information, DSI Holmes, I didn't invite you into my life and I don't appreciate you thinking you're going to tell me what to do. If you have a problem with me, I suggest you take it up with that constable who thought to make fun of me by assigning my case to you."

Holmes backed away, running his fingers through his thick, salt and pepper hair. "How much do you know about D/s relationships?"

"Excuse me?"

"Do you not understand the term?"

"Of course I do. I'm not some forty-year-old virgin. D is for dominance and S is for submission. What's your point?"

He signed, rubbing one hand across his full mouth and down his chin. "I don't doubt you know what the letters stand for," he said in a much calmer tone, "but how much do you know about the lifestyle?"

"Just things I've read. Also, Sage shared that she and Roark have one and that both you and Roark are Doms."

Holmes nodded. "Good. Roark's marriage to Sage is a damn good one and is D/s twenty-four/seven."

"I don't know what you're about to propose, DSI Holmes…"

He laughed. "I won't lie to you, Rachel—I've had a lot of unseemly mental images of you flashing through my mind since I met you. But I'm not about to strip off that flimsy nightgown, toss you over my knee and give you a good spanking. Though God knows, I think it would do you a world of good on a variety of levels."

He held his hand up to ward off her argument. "That was wildly inappropriate; I apologize." He gestured to the sofa and when she sat at one end, he sat at the other, putting reasonable space between them. "My point was that in D/s, the single most important thing between two people is open, honest communication. I can't help you if you keep holding things back."

"I didn't think they were important."

"Why don't you let me decide what's important? After all, you may have a doctorate, but I'm the detective—same first, last and number of letters, but totally different skill sets."

Rachel couldn't help but appreciate the detective's innate kindness, strength and authority. "You have a point. In my defense, I didn't want to sound silly or deranged from lack of sleep."

"I can see that. But as I said earlier, I believe something strange is going on. As I understand it, it began at the end of one of your tours. You went to close an open door and felt it being shut from the other side and then felt as though a cold wind passed through you. Do I have that right?"

"If I'm being completely honest, it was more than just a wind. It was like—you know when you experience a sudden unexplained shudder or shiver?"

Holmes nodded. "It's said that someone is walking over your grave."

"Exactly. That's what I experienced—an almost violent shudder and then the frightening idea that it was a portent of things to come. That someone was either coming to take me to my grave or walking over it."

"So when the door in your flat started opening…"

"But it was more than that," she interrupted, her body shivering slightly as she remembered how scared and alone she had felt—and how unable to move or even cry out. "My eyes were absolutely riveted to the spot, and I could actually see the deadbolt and the knob turn before the door opened. Then, the feeling of someone walking over my grave returned. It was very unsettling."

"I think, Dr. Moriarty, that is probably a gross understatement," said Holmes in a gentle tone, trying to reassure her.

Rachel looked up, allowing him to see her vulnerability. "All right, to be completely honest, it was terrifying. I haven't slept at night since. I can assure you,

Detective Holmes, there was no one there—either in my room or out on the balcony."

Holmes nodded his head and moved closer, taking her hands in his. "I believe you, Rachel. Something we can't yet explain is happening to you. I believe you are safer here at the Savoy where we can keep an eye on you. I have a great deal of unused leave and this afternoon, I arranged to take some of it. I want you to stay in the hotel and make sure that Roark, Gabe or I know where you are at all times. That way, we can protect you while we figure out what's happening and how to eradicate it from your life."

"I'm not used to answering to anyone. I gave that up when I lost—gave up my job at the university and moved to England."

Holmes smiled. "You're going to need to get used to doing as you're told, or you might find out a lot more about D/s relationships than you bargained for."

"What do you mean by that?" she asked, trying to withdraw her hands from his, but failing to do so.

"I mean precisely what you think I mean. Rachel, something, at best, is trying to get your attention and frighten you. At worst, it wants to do you harm. You came to the Yard looking for help, and I'm going to keep you safe whether you like it or not. That means from here on out, you do what I tell you or there will be punishment."

His gentle warning seemed to stop her dead in her tracks. There was an evil part of him that was just the tiniest bit sadistic. It rather hoped she'd defy him so he could show her how he dealt with disobedience.

Wait a minute! She isn't my sub. She isn't mine to discipline.

Still, his cock stiffened at the mental image that sprang too easily to mind of Rachel draped across his lap getting her bottom spanked. Oh, and all the delicious ways he could show her she'd been forgiven. God, how he envied Roark his relationship with Sage. It was well defined and so deeply satisfying to them both.

Rachel was deeply submissive; he'd bet his life on it. Even the mention of the word punishment had caused an uptick in her arousal. Her nipples had stiffened, and he was quite certain her pussy would be soft and wet if he reached between her legs. His cock pressed against the fly of his trousers, apparently of the opinion that he could discover just how ripe and ready she was for plunder if he'd just carry her off to bed, stripping her of the nightgown that did little to conceal her voluptuous figure. He'd been right; Rachel's frumpy clothes hid her true beauty.

"Punishment?" she whispered, eyes wide, as if aroused. But she quickly recovered her nerve. "Did you just threaten me, Detective Holmes? Does the Yard know of your proclivities?"

"My proclivities? You mean that I hold Master status at Baker Street?" Holmes laughed. "Why yes, they do. In fact, several of my superiors also play at Baker Street. Look, Rachel, why don't I call Roark and ask him to bring me the leftovers? We can have dinner and then turn in."

Rachel sat up straight, arms crossed. "I have no intention of sleeping with you, detective. If that's the price of your services, I'd rather pay cash."

Ah, she was a feisty thing. Holmes liked that; he enjoyed disciplining a sub. It provided both parties with what they needed and wanted. But the idea of disciplining Rachel went far beyond an emotionless contract. From her, he wanted more. And he realized that was what was missing in his life. The connection, the emotion, was part and parcel of what Roark had with Sage. Holmes envied that. He wanted to experience in this life, this real mortal life, the sensuality and intimacy that came from training a sub to give herself over to him completely, submitting fully to his authority. And not just any sub.

Rachel. He wanted Rachel.

"If and when we sleep together, Rachel," he growled, "it will be because we both want it and will have nothing to do with the price of my services. But you mind what I said. From here on out, you do as you're told."

Before she could say anything more to provoke him, there was a knock on the door. Holmes went to answer it. In swept Gabe, who carried with him the take-out boxes from their favorite Indian restaurant.

"I decided it might be safer down here," he said by way of explanation.

"What's up?" asked Holmes.

"Apparently, Sage took exception to you hauling Rachel down the hall to your room and insisted Roark do something. Roark refused, and Sage decided both he and you were being arrogant assholes."

"She didn't include you?"

"Nope. I'm just the casual observer—forever on the outside looking in."

Holmes laughed. Gabriel Watson was one of the favorite Doms of Baker Street. Subs literally lined up to play with the man.

"You might want to leave the curry and go. I'm not so sure Rachel and I aren't about to have the same argument."

"There's not going to be an argument," Rachel announced. "Mr. Watson, if you'll be so kind as to call me a cab, I'll get dressed and meet you downstairs. Please let Sage know I'll have her nightgown laundered and returned to her."

Watson looked from her to Holmes and back again. "Dr. Moriarty, from what Roark shared with me, your flat isn't safe. There's no way we're going to allow you to return there until it is. You can snarl and rail at the world all you like, but from this point forward your safety is in our hands—predominantly, Holmes'. Trust me when I tell you that we will keep you safe."

Her spine stiffened. "I haven't done anything wrong or illegal. You cannot hold me against my will."

"Would you like to place a wager on that?" asked Holmes. "Gabe, I may need to make some arrangements to ensure Rachel's safety and compliance. Roark and I need to go out in the morning."

"I'll keep an eye on both of them. I rather suspect Sage may well be looking for a way to even the score with Roark come daylight. Well, I'll leave you to it." Gabe left them, chuckling as he went.

"What did you mean by that?" she asked suspiciously.

"Exactly what I said. If you can't convince me that you'll behave and stay put, I will ensure that you're here upon my return. Since I didn't know what you liked, I got both red and green curry. What's your poison?" he said, removing the takeout containers from the bag, opening the disposable eating utensils and setting it all out on the table.

"Just like that? You can't really expect me to just go along with this, can you? Let me assure you I won't."

"Yes, you will. I want you to think about two things before you act out tomorrow. First, I don't make idle threats. Second, I'm one of the best disciplinarians at Baker Street. Now—red or green?"

Rachel looked as if she wanted to spew all kinds of venom in his direction but thought better of it. He'd have to wait to see if common sense overtook pride before deciding how to deal with her come morning.

"Red."

He grinned. "My kind of woman."

As they sat sharing what Holmes hoped would be the first of many dinners together, Rachel began to relax. And so did he.

"What prompted you to move to England?" he asked, around a savory bite of the delicious curry. "I can't imagine you had a sudden, overwhelming desire to drag people around and try to educate them."

She smiled. "I've always been an educator in one form or another. Most of the people who sign up for my tours are looking for something more in-depth than they can find with one of the big tour companies."

"Rachel, you should know I've been a detective and a Dom for a very long time. Both require a man to read people's body language and to pick up on subtle signals as to what they're thinking and planning to do. Want to know what else good cops and Doms have in common?"

"A penchant for violence?" she said silkily.

"Ouch. And no; just the opposite. Both require

someone who at their core has a need to serve and protect. I'm at the top of my game in both areas."

"Want to enlighten me as to what you mean by that?"

Holmes leaned closer to her. "People have tells when they're not being honest. When you're considering shading the truth, you chew on your lower lip—well, not really chew, but kind of nibble at it. So, whatever you're thinking about leaving out of your answer about moving to England, don't. When I ask you a question, I want a simple, straightforward answer."

"And if I choose not to answer? Or answer in a way you don't find satisfactory?"

"Then you'll find out exactly what it is you want to know."

"And what, pray tell, is that?"

"What it feels like to answer to a man's authority. To feel him put you over his knee and pepper your pretty backside with a spanking that puts such a sting in your tail, you'll make a better decision next time."

CHAPTER 5

Rachel feared Holmes was right. When he talked about discipline and answering to his authority, it didn't disgust her at all. Rather, the very idea sent a jolt of arousal through her system—like none she'd ever felt before. When she'd first met him, she'd chalked up the intensity of her attraction to the fact that since she'd been in England, the only pleasure she'd had was by her own hand. She'd always been careful and had followed a strict code of ethics and morality when dealing with her students.

But that hadn't saved her. It had merely left her isolated. When the scandal had hit, she had been completely unprepared. The fact that the baseless accusations had no merit seemed unimportant to everyone but her. A wealthy student whose grade she'd refused to raise in exchange for a not insubstantial sum of cash had accused her of having an affair with him and deliberately failing him when he'd broken it off. The fact that he hadn't done any of the work, had never managed better than a D on a test, and offered no proof of assignation seemed not to matter at all.

Holmes' gaze rested on her, fixing her in place with its intensity. "What are you thinking about right now, Rachel? I would appreciate it if you wouldn't try to test the limits of my patience with you. If you'd like to be spanked or explore D/s, I'd be more than happy to do that with you once we figure out what's going on. But I'm warning you for the last time, don't equivocate with me."

"Fine. You'll most likely run a background check and find out anyway. I came to England to get away from a rather nasty, salacious scandal."

"You were involved with drugs or a married man?"

She laughed. "At the risk of sounding bitter—no. My job and reputation probably could have survived either of those."

Holmes put down his plate, took a long sip of his select microbrew and said, "Tell me."

"Not much to tell. I had a relatively happy childhood until my parents were killed when I was a teenager. I spent a couple of years in the foster care system until I was able to get an emancipated minor status and went to work at the racetrack. I worked my ass off, got my GED and went to the university."

"Where you again worked your ass off, I guess."

In spite of herself, she smiled. He really was quite charming when he wasn't saying things that should have turned her completely against him, but instead only made him more compelling. She was like a moth to his flame. *Be careful*, she reminded herself. Get too close, and her wings might not only get singed, but consumed altogether.

"I did," she confessed. "I went to all the right faculty gatherings, volunteered for all the right committees; I even managed to publish all the right articles in all the right scholarly tomes."

"And some asshole with a dick destroyed your carefully constructed life."

She nodded. "I was accused of having an affair with a student and then failing him when he broke it off. Don't make light of it. The claims and the things he said were deeply humiliating, but worse yet was that no one really believed him. I became a liability, and it was more expedient to simply get me to leave. I loved my job and I worked hard for what I had, and his baseless claims wreaked havoc on my life."

"They believed him over you? Were you tenured?"

She nodded. "Yes, but gross misconduct negates that."

"But you didn't do it."

"You don't know that."

"Yes, I do. How'd he pull it off? No, wait, let me guess—Daddy had a lot of money and even more pull with the governing body. They allowed you to resign and gave you enough money for you to leave and start your own company."

"I suppose you think I sold out," she said, wondering why it had lifted her spirits when he never even considered that she might have done it. And why, she wondered, did it threaten to crush her heart if he condemned her for taking the only course she thought she had available?

"On the contrary. You looked at the situation, saw the cards were stacked against you and chose to make the best out of a bad situation." He leaned forward, once more taking her hands in his. "I'm so sorry that happened to you, Rachel. Give me their names and I'll get them put on a no-fly list. It won't hold up, but it'll cause them all kinds of hell the next time they try to get on a plane."

"Could you do that?" He nodded, grinning. "I don't want you to, but that's a lovely thought. You didn't even consider that it might be true."

"No, I didn't. Time for a little straightforward truth. I am wildly attracted to you, Rachel. I don't think I've ever felt called to a woman the way I am to you. Whether or not you know it or want to admit it, you're a submissive by nature."

"I'm not weak."

He laughed. "And therein lies the biggest misconception about submission. It takes an incredibly strong individual to admit they need the peace that comes with submission. You'll hear those who live the lifestyle talk about power exchange. Outsiders think that means the sub exchanges her weakness for his strength, but it won't work if both individuals aren't strong. What a sub offers is her softness, not weakness; she offers her trust in exchange for her Dom serving her needs and cherishing her gift."

He shook his head. "Listen to me go on. Sorry."

"Don't apologize. I never thought about it in terms like that. You make it seem kind of dreamy. Sometimes I have so many thoughts and emotions whirling around in my head…" she said, sitting back with a sigh.

"A little peace—a place where you don't have to do anything but surrender, revel in just being, and delight in the pleasure your Dom can give you—doesn't sound too bad?"

"Bad? Sounds like heaven."

"It can be. But you can't keep secrets from each other."

The way he talked made it seem divine. But could she truly give herself over to him that way? She wondered what it would be like to trust someone that completely, to know they were looking out for your best interests and keep you safe. She hadn't felt that with anyone since her parents had died. She realized how much she had missed it.

"Why don't you sleep on it?" he suggested. "You take the bed…"

"No, Holmes, I'm much smaller than you. I can curl up on the couch."

"How about we try it my way? How about you do what I tell you?"

"Do women always do what you tell them to?" she teased.

"Usually, unless they're being a brat."

"Don't you think I could be a brat?"

He laughed. She liked the sound of his laugh—so strong, melodious and full of humor. "I think you could be a glorious brat if you had a mind to. Fact is, you're the only woman I've ever met that I believe could rival Sage in bad behavior."

She was intrigued and flattered. "Do you really?"

"I do. In fact, you might actually be worse. Sage can be incredibly impulsive and often doesn't consider all of the consequences of something before she decides to defy Roark. I think you'd examine all the angles and get away with a whole lot of shit I never found out about."

Rachel sat back, feeling inordinately happy about Holmes thinking she could misbehave so wonderfully.

"But before you fall in love with the idea of being naughty, you should know one thing."

"What's that?" she quipped.

"There are consequences for misbehaving. And while your mind might dismiss that as negligible, I assure you, your ass will not thank you for it."

The deep, seductive tenor of Holmes' voice as he

hinted at spanking her thrilled her. She imagined he could damn near talk a woman to orgasm. How she'd love to put that thought to the test.

"What if… what if I was interested in exploring something like this?"

Holmes studied her closely. "If, after you've thought it over, you'd like to explore my lifestyle, I'd be honored to show you. But we'll have a contract that spells out exactly what we expect and are agreeing to. It not only makes it clear, but it protects both of us."

This time it was her turn to take his hands in hers. "I was making an idle threat. Your sex life is your own. Having false accusations made about mine, I'm the last person who would hold someone's choices against them. I would never report you."

He laughed again. "It wouldn't do you any good. As I said, Baker Street boasts a number of members who are with the Yard, including a couple of my superiors."

"Fine, but I just wanted you to know. And thank you for believing me—not just about whatever is going on, but about what brought me here to England."

"You're welcome. Go to bed, Rachel, and leave the door open. I'll be right out here." As she turned toward the bedroom, he called out to her. "And Rachel?" She stopped and looked at him. "My protecting you is *not* dependent on you deciding to move forward with something more than a bodyguard/detective and protectee relationship."

"Thank you, Holmes. For the record? I never thought it did."

Once inside her bedroom, she walked over to the door leading out to the balcony, checking the lock, before turning back the bed covers. All the while, she thought about what Holmes had said. She wasn't ignorant of BDSM. In fact, she often felt that some of the more erotic romance books were closer to what had gone on in the time of the Tudors. Her first foray into romance books had led her to Sage Matthews' works, which were decidedly rich and graphic in detail, character development and storyline.

The thought of Holmes in a pair of leather trousers, naked above the waist, showing off his brawny chest and muscular physique as he helped her to sit at his feet on a pillow did wonderfully arousing things to her body. It had been so long, she'd begun to think that part of her life was over and the only passion she'd find was in books. Being in the presence of DSI Michael Holmes made her blood, not to mention her heart and her nether region, pound.

Smiling she closed her eyes and went to sleep. She wasn't sure how long she'd been out, but a quiet scratching at the glass door out to the balcony caused her to sit up in bed. Just like in her flat, she saw the handle to the deadbolt move, twisting open. She tried to scream, but no sound came out. The door opened, and the temperature of the room dropped. Rachel wanted to move, to do something, but she felt frozen in place.

When she felt the mattress sink down, as if some creature had landed beside her, she finally found her voice. With a shriek, she turned on whatever it was that had joined her in the room.

"Easy, Rachel. It's just me," Holmes murmured. "Is that it?" He nodded toward the door, where the room seemed strangely blurred.

"I don't have my glasses on or my contacts in, but it feels like it," she whispered, settling her back against his chest as his arms came around her protectively. She was still terrified, but a lot less so within Holmes' embrace.

"It isn't your eyesight. Whatever it is, is just hanging there in the air, just to the left of the door. I can see through it, but it's like the very air is out of focus. Everything around it looks normal."

"So you can see it too? I mean, as much of it as there is to see?"

He tightened his arms around her. "Yes, sweetheart. I can see it."

"It followed me here, Holmes. What am I going to do?"

"You're going to do what I tell you and let me handle this. What does it normally do?"

"It just hangs there, doing nothing. Sometimes I

think I can hear it breathing, and the other night I thought I heard it say something."

"As if it was trying to speak to you?"

"No, just one word."

"What was the word?"

"Whore."

CHAPTER 6

Tightening his arm around her, Holmes reached for the house phone and called the suite next door.

"Roark? Get your ass out of bed and get down here. Whatever it is that's got Rachel spooked followed her to the Savoy."

"Don't you have a gun?" she whispered.

"I don't think a bullet is going to stop it. But whatever happens, I'm here. You are not alone, and I am not going to let whatever it is have you."

Holmes' deep voice commanded and soothed at the same time. There was comfort to be found in that voice and in the arms wrapped around her.

The next thing she knew, the door to their suite flung open and both Gabriel and Roark burst into the bedroom, throwing the electric switches and flooding the space with light. There was a whoosh as the curtains ruffled, the balcony door slammed shut and the lock relatched itself.

"What the fuck?" said Gabe.

Roark headed toward the door. "I need to go check on Sage. We'll be right back. Gabe, order up a pot of coffee and something to eat." He darted out.

Holmes looked over his shoulder, shielding Rachel's body from Gabe. He knew it was ridiculous —they hadn't even sketched out a contract—but he felt fiercely protective of the woman in his arms.

"You want to give us some privacy so Rachel can put on some clothes?" he growled.

"Sure, but I think she looks lovely in that nightgown," teased Gabe.

"I think you'd find it hard to do security work if I put your eyes out."

Laughing, Gabe left the room.

"Don't you think you should go with him?" she asked, suddenly aware of just how exposed she was in the thin negligee.

"Sweetheart, I've already spent time ogling you in that less than nothing nightie. And Gabe is wrong. You don't look lovely; you look gorgeous. You are an incredibly beautiful woman, Rachel. Besides, do you really want me to leave you alone?"

She smiled. "You have a point, but I am going to slip into the bath to pull something on."

"That's fine for tonight, but you should know, if

you sign that contract, you'll be spending a lot of time naked."

"Why?" she asked, a note of open curiosity in her voice.

"Because you are stunning and seeing you naked would please me."

"Is this one of those Dom things?"

Holmes grinned. "It is indeed."

She wasn't sure how or why, but Holmes' easy banter reassured her and made her feel sexy too. He thought she was gorgeous? Had he looked in the mirror? The man was drool-worthy. Well over six feet, close to six-six if she had to guess. Broad shoulders that led to a cut chest and a set of six pack abs. He had removed his shirt and had rushed in wearing only his trousers. Earlier, those trousers had been tented—and from the outline of the cock contained in them, the man was well-hung.

"Do you always sleep in your trousers?" she called from the bath.

"Only when I'm sleeping on a lady's couch instead of her bed."

Rachel came out wearing a pair of leggings and a sweater.

"You could at least have been comfortable in your boxers. Or do you prefer tighty-whiteys?"

"Keep it up, brat. If you want a spanking, just ask for one. If you do, I'll make sure you enjoy it. Provoke me to the point you've earned yourself some discipline, and I can assure you, you won't."

Her chin came up. "I haven't signed a contract yet. Haven't even agreed to give this a try."

Holmes rolled off the bed like a large panther getting up from his kill. He kissed the tip of her nose and grinned. "Haven't you?"

Pointing her toward the door, he swatted her ass. The stroke propelled her forward and delivered enough sting that she could feel the imprint from his hand and the resulting heat that radiated out. She blushed.

Moments later, she was in the main room, where the others waited. Sage rushed over, throwing her arms around her. "Rachel, are you all right? What a stupid question—of course you aren't. Roark said the thing was weird. Was it a ghost, do you think?"

Rachel shook her head. "I don't know. It has no discernable shape."

"Is this the first time you've seen it?" asked Roark.

"No. She's seen it before and I think has from the beginning, haven't you?" Holmes glowered at her. "We are going to have a specific clause about your penchant for holding back information."

"I'm sorry. I just didn't want to believe I was dealing with something supernatural. I've heard a kind of breathing noise from the beginning, as if it's wheezing. The last couple of nights, it's tried to speak."

"It managed that tonight," said Holmes, scowling.

"What did it say?" asked Sage, grabbing a notebook and scribbling down notes.

"Sage? What have I told you about treating meetings with clients like a data finding mission for a future novel?" asked Roark in a kind but stern tone.

"Not to," she said, placing the notebook in his outstretched hand. "Sorry, Rachel. Roark's right, it's a bad habit."

Rachel smiled. "It's all right. I guess that answers my question about why your books are so vividly detailed."

Gabe chuckled. "You two are so screwed," he said to Roark and Holmes. "I've let the staff know I'm here and they're sending up food, coffee and tea."

Once the food had been delivered, they all settled down to talk more calmly. Holmes took up residence on one end of the couch. When Rachel brought him a cup of hot tea, he opened his arm. "Sit with me."

Rachel curled up on the couch beside him, more content and relaxed than she had been in a long time. Holmes was incredibly seductive, yet oddly reassuring. That thing might have followed her, but at least it hadn't hovered over her like it had before. Holmes' presence seemed to have made it a little less bold—and Rachel had to admit that it had become bolder over time.

"What are you thinking?" Holmes asked.

"I just realized I hadn't told you something—not

because I was holding it back, but because I just didn't think to." He nodded. "The first night, that thing barely came into the room. In fact, it felt like it was partly in and partly out. But each night since, it's come closer and closer. The last night at my flat, it crowded me into the back of the chair and then hovered over me, as if it was leaning down trying to intimidate me—or frighten me to death."

"That could be significant," said Holmes. "I'll get Eddy to start looking into it."

"Who's Eddy? Someone at the Yard? I don't want them thinking I'm some nutcase."

"Eddy Chastain is a friend of ours—a hacker," said Holmes, reassuringly.

"Sage, don't you have a minor character in the Clive Thomas books who's a hacker named Eddy?" asked Rachel.

Sage glanced at Roark and Holmes. "Yes. I bug him about a lot of things. It's kind of my homage to him. A thank-you. He does a lot of work for Roark and Holmes on occasion."

"That's sweet," said Rachel, snuggling back into Holmes' comforting embrace.

Holmes settled his arms around her. "Anything else you can think of?"

"No—that's it. I really did forget about the whole hovering thing and honestly, I thought I was imagining that part."

"You accept that whatever it is exists, but not that it is getting bolder and more threatening?"

"I couldn't deny that it was unlocking and opening the door. I watched it, but you saw it—whatever it is—or at least what you can see of it." She shivered against him, enjoying the heat that rolled off his body.

He kissed her temple—a sweet, intimate touch that reassured her. "We'll figure it out. First we need to know what it is. Then we need to figure out how to make it leave you alone."

"It didn't seem to like you," she said. "I mean, it called me a whore, but it seemed afraid of you and Roark—you more than Roark."

Roark nodded. "I agree. Male energy, perhaps?"

"I think it's attached itself to you somehow," said Holmes. "Did you pick up anything in that room? Even something innocuous?"

Rachel shook her head. "Nothing. I am very careful on my tours not to disturb anything. It's how I get clients into places no one else can. If it's attached to me, then until you get rid of it, I won't be able to sleep."

"If it's afraid of Holmes, I suggest you start sleeping with him sooner rather than later," said Roark.

Sage jabbed him in the ribs with her elbow. "You'll have to forgive him. He can be a bit of a caveman."

"For God's sake, are we all going to sit around here pretending they're not going to end up in bed together? And they'll be doing a lot more than sleeping. Sage," he growled, "you get the first jab. The next one gets you spanked. Besides, the thing is afraid of Holmes, so the closer she is to him, the better."

Rachel settled back against him. "I think Roark is right."

"Does it come back?" asked Gabe.

"No. It usually stays longer but once it leaves, it leaves."

"Does it have a usual time?" asked Roark.

"Hmm," Rachel said, thinking. "Now that I think about it, it's usually around two or three in the morning."

"The witching hour," said Sage. At Rachel's confused look, she continued, "They say that's when the boundary between the two planes of existence is at its weakest."

"So you think I'm being haunted?"

"I think, sweetheart," said Holmes, "that some kind of energy has attached itself to you and finds it easiest to get at you when the veil is the thinnest."

"It's always gone before the sun comes up, if that helps," she said.

"Speaking of which," said Roark as he stood, scooping Sage up into his arms, "what do you say we get a little sleep. Holmes? You still up for a visit to Mary Kelly's later?"

"Absolutely. That's where this thing started. Rachel and I need to talk about a few things first, including whether or not I can trust her to stay put while we're gone."

"I don't think I like the sound of that," Rachel said, trying to make it sound lighthearted.

"Good. Then I won't have to explain it to you. Go sit on the bed and wait for me."

Gabe headed toward the door. "I'm going to go check in with my staff and try to catch a nap. Let me know what you need me to do," he said.

Both he and Roark, who was still cradling Sage to his chest, left them alone. Hurrying into the bedroom, Rachel quickly changed back into the nightgown Sage had loaned her and sat on the edge of the bed. She wasn't sure what she expected or what she even wanted. She could hear Holmes talking to someone on the phone, presumably Eddy.

A few minutes later, Holmes entered the room. As soon as he saw that she was waiting for him so obediently, he nodded in approval. "Good girl."

Rachel flushed. Why was it those two words rolled over her with a warmth she'd never experienced before?

"I want you to try and get some sleep," he ordered. "I've got some work I want to do before Roark and I go to Mary Kelly's."

"Do you want me to come with you?" she asked.

"No, sweetheart, but thank you. While I'm gone, I

don't want you to leave this room. If you and Sage want to get together, you can go to her suite, order from room service, or there are a bunch of places that deliver. Am I clear?"

She nodded. "I might point out to you, I haven't signed the contract yet."

"I'm aware. I'll call Baker Street and have my normal contract modified and sent over to you here at the hotel. You can look it over while I'm gone."

"You have a normal contract?"

"Yes. Remember what I told you. D/s is about open, clear communication between partners and sets out their expectations, needs and limits. My normal contract is very clear that we are just playing and that I'm not looking for any kind of commitment."

"Oh," she said, feeling as though he'd just ground her heart under his heel, which was ridiculous as she'd only met the man yesterday.

He lifted her chin, smiling down at her. "That clause will be removed. And I have several others I want added, including one about exclusivity…" He paused, gazing at her. "…And one that says you are not allowed to play with yourself unless I want you to, for my enjoyment."

Rachel could feel the heat from the blush that was staining her cheeks. "What if I want something or don't want something?"

"That's what the contract is for sweetheart—negotiation."

CHAPTER 7

When Rachel couldn't seem to settle in the bedroom by herself, Holmes joined her. Stretching out on the bed, he leaned against the headboard and worked on his computer, while she dozed. She seemed to find comfort in his presence, snuggling up next to him with her hand on his thigh. He stroked her hair whenever she seemed to become restless.

Once the sun had kissed the sky, he eased off the bed and went into the other room to order breakfast.

"Did you sleep at all last night?" she asked, standing in the doorway with nothing on but his shirt.

"Not much, but I don't require a lot of sleep. I just ordered breakfast. I can call back down and add to the order, but I probably ordered more than I need. We could share."

She nodded. "I'd like that. Thank you for last

night and for all of this."

"I'm happy to do it. I need you to look over that contract while I'm gone and stay here in our room or with Sage in theirs."

"Whatever that thing is, it doesn't seem to manifest itself during the day."

"Good to know, but the order remains the same. Don't leave this floor. You and Sage can keep each other company, but you are not to incite each other into disobedience."

"But I need my laptop. I have things I'm working on for upcoming tours. I still have a business to run."

"You can use my laptop."

"It isn't the same. I've got files on there and programs specific to my company…"

"In that case, I can either swing back by your flat, or if you'd like to make sure you've got everything you need, you and I will go together when Roark and I get back from Mary Kelly's. That's probably best. If you'll look at what I packed for you while I'm gone, we can pick up whatever you need for a week or so."

"Holmes, I can't afford to stay at the Savoy even for a night, much less a week."

"Don't worry about that. I have it covered."

"I couldn't possibly let you," she protested softly.

Holmes drew her onto his lap, his mouth closing on hers. God, her mouth was sweet—like honeyed wine. At first she seemed uncomfortable, but as his lips teased hers—coaxing, persuading, seducing—she sighed and melted into him, her arms coming up around his neck. He'd been playing at Baker Street on a regular basis since he'd come out of the book. It was safer. The only people who knew about his, Roark and Felix's origins were the three of them and Sage—the woman who had created them. He was grateful she'd given him family money, good investments and a big dick—the latter coming to life as Rachel settled onto his thighs.

He ran his tongue along her lower lip, teasing, and her mouth softened and opened for him. It was all he could do not to take command and invade her mouth, conquering it and bending her to his will. His tongue slid along hers as one hand cradled her head and face, while his other arm wrapped around her to keep her in place. Normally, he didn't kiss the women he had sex with at Baker Street—it seemed too intimate, too much of a commitment. But with Rachel, he craved both.

Holmes might have taken things further—lack of contract be damned—had room service not shown up just then to deliver their meal. Annoyed at the interruption, he reluctantly relinquished her mouth and set her on the sofa. He opened the door and had the waiter put the tray on the credenza before leaving.

"You know, we could go back to my place and save the expense of the hotel," she offered.

He'd need to teach her that he meant to make a habit of spoiling her and that she didn't need to worry about what things cost. Idly, he wondered how long he should wait before moving her into his home. Sage might have written that he'd been born in the West End, but she'd given his character a townhome in Chelsea right across from the River Thames. It had a beautiful Victorian façade, cobblestone street and small back garden. It was actually far too large and grand for him alone, but with Rachel there with him, the ample space would be ideal.

What the hell is wrong with me? I barely know the woman—we haven't even had sex—and I'm already moving her into my home.

"I can get one of the paper plates from last night, and I think there were a couple of extra forks," said Rachel as he brought the tray to the coffee table in front of the sofa.

"Not necessary," he rumbled, watching the way her body responded just to the sound of his voice. Her body seemed to soften, with the slightest shiver of desire and an uptick in the scent of her arousal. Holmes sat back down and pulled her into his lap, wondering what she'd do if he simply slipped his hand between her legs. "I prefer you sit with me. You hold the plate, and I'll feed us."

Rachel blushed but settled herself pleasantly against his thighs. They were sharing breakfast when Roark joined them. When she tried to disengage herself, Holmes tightened his arms around her, holding her until she settled again.

"I must say, Dr. Moriarty, you look rather fetching sitting on Holmes' lap in his shirt. I wish I could offer to come back later so you two could take a bit more time this morning, but the person who manages Mary Kelly's room is expecting us, so we need to get a move on."

"Besides which," drawled Holmes, "he's already had his way with Sage this morning."

"One of the many advantages to being a happily married man—especially when one's spouse is an erotic romance writer."

Rachel laughed, and Holmes felt her body completely relax against his. "Maybe you can persuade him that I am perfectly capable of going to my flat to get my laptop and some additional clothes."

"That won't happen, sweetheart. Number one rule among Doms—never come between a Dom and his sub."

"I keep telling you, I haven't signed a contract yet."

Roark chuckled. "If you think he needs a contract to make you his sub, you haven't been paying attention. Holmes, put the girl on the sofa, and let's get on our way. Rachel, good to see you looking better than you did last night."

Holmes shook his head and set Rachel down next to him. "My laptop doesn't have a password," he told her, "so help yourself. I don't think we'll be overly long."

Before leaving, Holmes kissed her again, and admonished her to behave. Then, he and Roark took the elevator to the lobby. The valet had already brought Holmes' car around. It was a typical, dreary, damp London kind of day and he was glad of the Savoy's covered entrance area.

"I'm surprised you're deigning to ride in my SUV," he quipped.

"As you once pointed out to me, it has that sticker indicating it's a police vehicle, which means we can park wherever the hell we like."

They got in the vehicle, and Holmes pulled out into the London traffic.

"After lunch, Rachel wants to go back to her place. I really should have remembered her laptop. She'll also need a few more things. I'm not so sure this is going to be as quick and easy as I originally thought. I thought about taking her to Chelsea, but if I have to leave her there, she'd be alone. I don't feel comfortable doing that."

"Because you think this creature means her harm? Or because you need to control the narrative?"

"What do you mean by that?"

"Sage pointed out to me that before you let this thing go too far with Rachel—and Sage and I both believe she couldn't have written a better partner for you—you need to tell her the truth about our origins."

Holmes nodded. "I know. I thought about that this

morning as I was imagining a life with her. But I haven't a clue how to bring that up in a conversation. 'Oh by the way, until a year ago, I didn't exist outside the pages of Sage's books.' It's the same damn reason we haven't said anything to Gabe. I have to tell you, that's really starting to bug me. He's supposed to be one of my closest friends, and there's this enormous secret just lying there between us like the proverbial elephant in the room, although I'm the only one aware of it."

"I know. I feel the same way about Gabe, and so does Felix. Putting that aside for the moment, what did you make of that thing last night?"

Holmes looked over his shoulder, turning on the directional signal to change lanes, which in London could be a risky business. Most people feared London's notorious roundabouts, which were easily navigable by simply remembering that the only vehicles you needed to yield to was on your left. The danger in driving in London was the horrendous traffic. While not quite as bad as Rome, it easily rivaled Paris or New York City. The almost continual drizzle wasn't helping either.

"Weird. Rachel is clearly terrified. She couldn't even call for help. I just happened to hear the door open, and I knew damn well I'd closed and locked it and was pretty sure Rachel hadn't opened it."

"How did it react to you?"

"It seemed leery of me but was focused on Rachel

and her reaction. I've never seen anything like it, never even heard of anything like it. I did some research on Mary Kelly. Interesting woman. Very little is known about her, and what is known is of questionable veracity."

"I remember Sage saying that when she thought about doing a book that featured the Ripper."

"The other thing I did a bit of research on was ghosts and spiritual apparitions. Lot of contradictory information out there, so I contacted Eddy and asked him to see what he could find."

"You think there might be something more usable on the other side of the veil?"

"I figure it can't hurt. One of the few things that everyone seems to agree on was that Mary Kelly was Irish and came from a fairly unstable home. A couple of police reports from the time said she left her family when they accused her of being a witch."

"Now that, I hadn't heard," said Roark. "Where did you learn that, and do you think it's reliable information?"

"How reliable it is, is questionable. It was 1888, Victorian England. There was a strong belief in all matters spiritual."

"Do you think that thing is somehow connected to Jack the Ripper?"

"Don't you? It seems too coincidental that something happened that day at Mary Kelly's room, and then this thing starts dogging Rachel. It bothers me that it seems attached to her, not just a place."

"Agreed."

They pulled up to 13 Miller's Court, where a well-groomed woman who looked to be about fifty years of age was waiting for them. She seemed agitated, pacing back and forth at the street entrance to the covered alleyway.

"Mrs. McCarthy?" Holmes said, noting the woman's nervousness. He wondered if she was apprehensive about going into the room. Did she know what had happened to Sage? Had similar things happened before?

"Yes. May I see some ID?" she asked.

"Of course." Holmes showed her his Scotland Yard ID and when she looked toward Roark, he said, "This is Roark Samuels."

The woman smiled. "That fancy detective that lives at the Savoy with his wife, Sage Matthews?"

"One and the same," said Roark with a grin. Sage had written him as famous, the kind of person who showed up routinely on the society page, so he'd become used to being recognized.

"I just love your wife's books—so imaginative and sexy. Please come this way," said Mrs. McCarthy, gesturing for them to follow her into the building.

"I understand that you just manage the room?" Holmes asked.

"Yes, the owner likes to keep an arm's distance

from it. Since it's the last place the Ripper murdered anyone, the space has provided a tidy income stream for more than a century. We have regular visiting hours, but normally don't allow people inside. They can peek through the window or through the open door."

"But you let Rachel inside," said Holmes, noting her unwillingness to precede them as they approached the room in which Mary Kelly had been killed.

"Yes. We make an exception for Dr. Moriarty. She's so respectful and so careful. Can I ask why Scotland Yard and a famous detective want to see it?"

"Dr. Moriarty has received some threats, and as part of our investigation, I'm tracing her whereabouts for the past few weeks. Roark and I are having lunch later, and he expressed an interest in coming along," Holmes explained.

"I'm sorry to hear that. Dr. Moriarty is a nice lady. I hope you catch whoever is threatening her. I'd hate to see her get hurt."

Roark said, "I can assure you, Mrs. McCarthy, DSI Holmes will ensure that doesn't happen."

She nodded and pointed down the passage. "It's this way. They cleaned it up back in the day as best they could. You can still see faint blood stains. Back in the seventies, the owners had someone make replicas of the furniture and furnishings from the pictures of the crime scene. The cops took all the originals as evidence. The only thing they didn't replace is the mirror over the fireplace. It's old, heavy and bolted to the wall."

She ushered them through the twenty-six-foot-long archway to the door. Holmes watched as she seemed to steel herself before unlocking it and stepping back.

Holmes cracked open the door, then paused to look at her. "Would you like to accompany us?"

Mrs. McCarthy shook her head. "No, I don't go in there. The place gives me the willies. If it weren't for the salary the owner pays me and how close it is to my house, I'd never enter that cursed room again."

"Cursed?" asked Holmes.

"No one's ever said it, but I swear you can feel it. The place just isn't right. I won't even walk down the alleyway after dark. Did you ever see the original photos and drawings? Horrifying. I don't care what that poor woman did in her lifetime; no one deserves to die like that."

"Agreed," said Holmes. "I've always thought that at least he killed them before he started to carve them up."

Mrs. McCarthy crossed herself and stepped back as he and Roark entered the small, twelve-by-twelve room. From the doorway, you could see the entire space. You faced the back wall which had a small fireplace with, as Mrs. McCarthy had said, a mirror bolted to the wall. On the left was the infamous window through which the rent collector had spotted the body and under it, a table. Along the right wall was the bed where Mary Kelly had been carved up and left, almost like, Holmes had always thought, some kind of macabre science experiment gone horribly wrong. There was a hutch that flanked the fireplace on the right side and wainscotting all around the room. Mrs. McCarthy was right, it was eerie.

"Brr," said Roark as they crossed the threshold. "Do you have air conditioning in here?"

"No," said Mrs. McCarthy from the doorway. "That's what I mean. The room is always cold. Always."

Holmes handed a pair of latex gloves to Roark, then donned his own. They made their way around the room, careful not to disturb things but looking at their placement and comparing them to the crime photos Holmes had downloaded on his tablet.

"Everything seems to be here and in the right place," said Roark.

"Dr. Moriarty wouldn't steal," asserted Mrs. McCarthy.

"Of course not," said Holmes with a smile. "Rachel is very careful and respectful of history."

Standing in front of the fireplace, he noted a large crack in the polished obsidian that had served as a reflective surface in the days of Queen Victoria.

"I don't recall anything in the reports saying the mirror was damaged," said Holmes.

"Damaged?" asked Mrs. McCarthy. "The mirror

is original and old, but it's never been damaged. What's wrong with it?"

"There's a rather large crack in it. See?" He pointed at it, inviting her to take a closer look, but she refused to step across the threshold.

"I'll take your word for it. And that mirror has given me the creeps for years."

"How so?" asked Holmes.

"You'll think I'm off my rocker, but I swear it's ten degrees colder over there. More than once, when I wasn't looking at it, I felt as though someone was staring at me from the other side. But of course, when I turned back around, there was nothing there. Still, it chills me."

"Would you mind if I swabbed the crack and took some pictures?"

"No, you do what you need to do," said Mrs. McCarthy.

Holmes removed a sterile swab and container from his pocket and carefully ran the tip all along the crack before sealing it back in the evidence bag and marking it. Using his mobile phone, he took numerous pictures of the mirror and the room itself.

When he was finished, they thanked Mrs. McCarthy and made their way back to Scotland Yard's forensics unit where Holmes dropped off the swab and asked that they run tests on it as soon as possible. Next, they headed to Holmes' townhouse where he packed a larger bag. After debating, he decided to take his kit with him. When he turned to leave his closet, Roark was staring at him, grinning.

"You need to tell her. The further she gets involved, the angrier she'll be—not at what you tell her, but when it is you chose to do so."

"I know. I'm packing it just in case. I had my standard contract for play at Baker Street modified. Let's see if she's willing to sign it."

Roark shook his head. "You are so fucked."

As they got back in Holmes' vehicle, his mobile rang. He was surprised when he saw it was the lab.

"That was fast," he said. "Let me guess, you found nothing."

"No, but what I found was weird," said Joel Asheboro, one of the Yard's chief criminalists.

"What did you find?"

"We'll need to do further analysis, but you said you wanted it kept off the books, so I thought I'd give you some preliminary findings and do some more analysis when the lab is less crowded."

"What did you find, Joel?"

"It's what I didn't find. There's no DNA to speak of, but I did find nucleotides, which are its building blocks. And then I found something I can only describe as dark matter." The voice on the other end of the phone paused, then came back sounding tense. "Holmes, is this some kind of joke? And if not, what the hell are you involved in?"

CHAPTER 8

Rachel felt restless and bored. She'd been doing research on the wine cellar of Cardinal Wolsey, the man who had failed to get King Henry VIII a divorce from Catherine of Aragon. The cellar was intact and virtually untouched since the time of the Tudors. Special permission was required to gain entrance, and few were allowed to tread the same floors where the cardinal and the king were once said to have walked.

It would be a perfect location for a private tour, once she was back to normal business.

Earlier, she'd spoken to Sage only to realize the author had a pressing deadline, and Rachel was loathe to take her away from her work. So, since she was in negotiation with the government to take a small group into the cellar as part of her tour, Rachel got down to her own work. Pulling up her email on

Holmes' computer, she was about to begin the arduous process of filling out the necessary forms.

A knock on the door interrupted her. She looked out the peephole and recognized Gabriel from the night before. In his hands, he held an envelope.

Opening the door, she gestured for him to come in. "Hello, Gabriel. I want to thank you again for last night."

"Don't mention it. Roark and Holmes are two of my closest friends. There is very little I wouldn't do for them," he said, entering her suite.

Unlike the others in the group, Watson seemed aloof and a bit suspicious, as his eyes darted around the room as if assessing its contents—and her. What could he think she possibly had to gain in making up this story?

"I assure you, I don't want to see either of them hurt, but they both appear to be well-versed in how to defend themselves."

"From whatever it is that's got you spooked? I agree. Two of the most capable fighters I've ever known; both excellent marksmen. But both a bit too chivalrous, if you ask me."

"I'm afraid I don't understand."

"As I understand it from Felix, we send quite a bit of business your way. I would hate to see your business negatively impacted if our recommendation of your tours was lost because of something unseemly."

"Again, I think you have me at a disadvantage.

Why don't you tell me straight out what the problem is?"

Gabe nodded. "Yesterday, I did a quick background check on you, Dr. Moriarty. I'm not sure why it wasn't done before."

"Did Holmes ask you to do that?"

"No. But it occurred to me when this contract was delivered from Baker Street that I'm afraid Holmes is getting in over his head."

"You read the contract?" she accused.

"Not this one specifically, but in this size envelope, the only thing Holmes might have ordered from Baker Street is a contract. As you aren't a sub at Baker Street, you wouldn't have a general contract with the club to cover whatever is going on with you and Holmes. That means Holmes had it prepared specifically for you and sent over for your review. If he was just planning to scene with you a couple of times, he'd have waited until this was cleared up, then introduced you at the club and either given you his standard contract or used the general one that Baker Street would have you sign. He didn't do that. He's here at the Savoy, playing house with you. And he has Baker Street send over a specialized contract."

"And your point is?" she said, feeling the icy fingers of dread coiling around her.

"You left your position as a tenured professor," he said somewhat menacingly, looming over her, "under a cloud of innuendo and suspicion. Want to tell me about that? Does Holmes know?"

It was obvious Watson was trying to be intimidating. He was about to find out that she might be frightened of some evil apparition of Jack the Ripper, but some hunky house detective didn't scare her in the least.

Straightening her spine, she went on the offensive, taking a step into his personal space. "To answer your questions: yes, Holmes knows and it's none of your damn business. Just to get it all out in the open and to assuage your curiosity, I'll tell you I was accused of inappropriate behavior by a little weasel with more money than brains. Specifically, he said we'd had a sexual relationship, which we hadn't, and that when he broke it off that I retaliated by flunking him. The truth was the little bastard didn't do any of the work, flunked most of the tests and then tried to bribe me.

He then concocted his little lurid fantasy and when I assessed my chances of actually coming out the winner in that scenario, I decided to take the money they offered to go away quietly. As you might guess, even the shadow of suspicion about a sexual scandal, especially with a female professor, is enough to keep said professor from ever getting to work in her chosen field again. By the way Mr. Watson, I did nothing wrong. I'm just pragmatic and decided I was better off to take the money. So, I did and moved to England and started my own business. Have I benefitted from the Savoy's recommendations? Yes. Am I willing to stand here and let you cast aspersions on my character or accuse me of—exactly what is it you're accusing me of?"

She ticked off items on her fingers as she spoke. "Let's see, am I the femme fatale trying to seduce your friend so I can blackmail him? He tells me he's pretty bulletproof in that area. Or maybe I went to Scotland Yard making a baseless claim—but for what? To garner publicity? But then there's that pesky whatever the hell it was that unlocked the balcony door last night and terrorized me just like it's done every night for over a week. Now, there's a good time. So, which is it, Watson?"

By the time she was done, Rachel was out of breath. At least he had the good grace to blush, a look that was a bit incongruous on a man of his size and stature.

Sheepishly, he handed her the sealed envelope. "My apologies, Rachel. Apparently I misjudged the entire situation, and I am deeply sorry. After what I saw last night, it's obvious that you are who and what you say you are, and that Holmes is responding to a true damsel in distress. He's a great white knight. And for what it's worth, I've never known him to have a special contract prepared. I hope you can forgive me."

Rachel shook her head and then laughed at the sullen, disappointed look he gave her. "I wasn't saying I can't forgive you. As you say, things taken out of context often lead to erroneous assumptions. Given what happened back in the States, I'm a little gun-shy of being accused of something, even when the accuser wants nothing for himself, but is trying to look out for a friend. If you can forgive me for snapping, I can forgive you for being an interfering asshole. Deal?" She offered him her hand.

Watson clasped and shook it, smiling as he did so. "Deal. For what it's worth, I think it's going to be entertaining watching Holmes take you in hand. He's one of the best men I've ever known. Look the contract over. If you have any questions before he gets back, just call down on the house phone."

"Thanks, Watson."

With that, he handed her the envelope and let himself out. Flipping through the contract, Rachel was surprised by its extensiveness. When she thought about it, though, she could see what Holmes meant when he said it protected both parties and set out exactly what each of them was agreeing to. It covered expectations, limitations, general health and pregnancy prevention. There were several pages of fetishes listed and the contract asked that the parties each indicate their level of interest, their level of experience, and whether or not each item was a hard or soft limit. The third column regarding experience was the easiest—none.

Some of the fetishes, she'd never heard of; she had no idea what they were. For a moment, she thought about calling Watson to ask him to explain what she was reading. But she decided it would be less embarrassing to simply look them up on the computer. Breathing deeply, Rachel sat down and went over the paperwork in detail. It spelled out that she was agreeing to be Holmes' sub on an exclusive basis for the duration of the contract, which could be terminated by either party at any time. Holmes was also agreeing to exclusivity, as well as providing for and protecting her. He had left open the question of sex, painting it as something they would mutually agree to.

That clause made her smile. If Holmes thought she didn't intend to have sex with him, he should think again. That hard cock she'd felt throbbing beneath her both times she'd been in his lap was being offered up as part of the deal, and she was going to take advantage of it. Once she'd gone over it, she signed her name and dated it before going back to the application process for Cardinal Wolsey's wine cellar.

Working through it, Rachel realized there was a great deal of information on her laptop at home that would save her a lot of time and trouble. It was late morning, and she doubted Holmes would be back before lunchtime. If she just ran home, she could get a lot of her work done as well as pick up some more clothes. True, he'd told her to stay put. And the contract had spelled out that for the duration of the contract, she was agreeing to submit to his authority. Willful disobedience would be punished.

Why that thought sent a shiver through her body was not something she wanted to consider at this time.

She reasoned that it was daylight, and her odd encounters only happened in the dead of night. So she shouldn't be in any danger. Still, she didn't want Holmes to worry, so she left a note attached to the signed contract.

Holmes,

I've read, completed and signed the contract. While I had to look up some of the terms, I have to admit I'm interested in exploring this kind of relationship with you.

I'm working on an application to get a small tour I'm planning into Cardinal Wolsey's actual wine cellar. A lot of what I need is on my laptop at home. Sage is busy, and you and Roark said you wouldn't be back until lunch.

As it seems silly for you to have to go back out just as you get here, I'm going to run home. I might even be back before you get here.

Rachel

She wondered if she ought to sign it 'love' or 'always,' but that seemed over-reaching and premature, even though she was pretty sure it was close to the truth.

Leaving the signed contract and note in a prominent place. Rachel slipped out of her room and took the elevator to the garage, avoiding the lobby. No use in announcing to Watson that she was about to disobey his buddy Holmes. She walked to the surface street, hailed a cab and headed to her flat.

As they pulled up, she asked the cab driver to wait, saying she'd only be a few minutes. She ran up the steps to her flat and paused before unlocking the door. What if she was wrong? What if the thing—whatever it was—was waiting for her? She shook her head. There was no reason to think that. It had never appeared during the day.

She entered her apartment and grabbed her laptop case, ensuring it contained her computer, power cord, extra battery and mouse. She laid the case next to her purse. Rachel then checked her fridge to see if there was anything she needed to toss out and could see it had already been done. She'd have to thank Holmes for that.

Entering the walk-in closet she'd had built when she moved in, Rachel grabbed a large suitcase and packed her things, including two fancier dresses so that if they wanted to go to the Savoy for dinner, she wouldn't be underdressed. She was just about to head out the door when she remembered that when she'd looked at Baker Street's discreet website, it had indicated that fetish wear was required.

That could prove to be a problem. Given her earlier research, she didn't have anything that would be classified as appropriate. She looked up corset shops close by and saw a sponsored ad for The Dark Garden. She called the number.

"Dark Garden, this is Louis. May I help you?"

"Hi. My name is Rachel Moriarty…"

"Who is your Dom?"

Taken aback, she recovered quickly and went on the offensive. "What makes you think I'm not a Domme."

He chuckled. "Because my store caters to male Doms and female subs. As you are obviously female, I would need the name of your Dom. In fact, I would need him to call to set the appointment."

"That's ridiculous and might even be illegal. You can't discriminate like that."

"I don't think of it as discrimination. I simply know who my ideal customer is, and I don't waste my time or anyone else's offering myself up to be anything other than who I am."

"What if I want to surprise him?"

"I would be unable to help you in that regard. In my shop, your Dom makes all the decisions, including whether or not you will shop here. I suggest you have him call me back to book an appointment."

"People actually put up with your bullshit?" Rachel asked incredulously.

"Not only do they put up with it, but they sometimes wait months for an appointment. Good day to you. I suggest you let your Dom know that you are interested in coming here."

He didn't wait for her reply. He simply ended the call.

Rachel stared down at the phone. *We'll be going to Dark Garden, and I will let that shopkeeper know exactly what I think of his stupid policies.*

She gathered her things and went out to the waiting cab, which took her back to the Savoy. Rachel walked down from the street into the parking lot and back up the elevator to their floor. How easy it was becoming for her to think of it as their floor! She unlocked and opened the door only to find Holmes waiting for her—signed contract and her note in hand.

"Holmes, I thought I'd beat you back."

"I'm sure you did. Are you all right? Did anything happen?"

"No. I told you, it doesn't come after me during the day. It was fine. I noticed you cleaned out the fridge. Thank you for that."

"You're welcome. You're sure you read and understand the contract?"

"Yes."

He looked through the contract. "Your safeword is Tudor?" She nodded. "Are you choosing to use your safeword at this time?"

"Why on earth would I need my safeword?"

"Did you not see or understand the clause that

lays out how you will obey me, and when you don't there will be discipline?"

"Of course, I did. I don't sign documents without fully reading and understanding them."

"Good. Then I believe we should begin in the same manner as we will proceed. I want you to strip naked and go sit on the bed. In the future, once you have learned proper protocol, when you're going to be punished, I will expect you to be naked, kneeling on the floor or the bed with your legs spread wide and your hands resting on your thighs."

"You're planning to spank me?" she squeaked.

He nodded. "I am. I was very clear in what I expected of you while I was gone. I was also clear both before I left and in the contract that there would be consequences for disobeying me, which in most cases is a sound spanking. You just confirmed that you read and understood the contract before you signed it. You chose to flout my authority and are about to have your first taste of discipline. Get naked and get in that bedroom—now."

CHAPTER 9

"You can't be serious," she said.

"I can and I am. I understand that this is all new to you," he said calmly, rolling up the sleeve to his shirt, "but D/s is important to me and not just as a way to have sex. It's part and parcel of who I am. If we're going to try and make something out of whatever seems to be between us, you need to understand that. Your note said you wanted to give that a try. Were you lying to me?"

"No. I just didn't think… I mean, technically the contract wasn't in place before I disobeyed you."

Holmes nodded. "True enough, but I'm not going to play hyper-technical games with you. You don't have to do this. I understand D/s isn't for everybody, and that's perfectly okay. I will still keep you safe and figure out what this thing is and how we get rid of it. But you need to decide now what it is you want from me. If we're going to try and make a go of it, then you'll go into the bedroom, strip and wait on the bed for me to come in, put you over my lap and spank you. You're going to do that because that's what subs do—they submit themselves to their Dom's authority. That doesn't mean you don't have input into things, or that you can't disagree with me or even argue your position. What it does mean is that at the end of the day, you trust me to look after you."

"It seems rather lopsided to me. I understand what I get, but what do you get out of it?"

"An inordinate amount of satisfaction, and not just the sexual kind, although we should talk about that…"

"Look, Holmes," she said, searching for the right words but being distracted by the sight of him slowly rolling up the sleeves to his shirt, revealing muscular forearms. "I'm wildly attracted to you. I'd begun to think that my sex life had been put into permanent mothballs, but one look at you and it sprang back to life. So if we're putting our cards on the table, let me be clear—I want to have sex with you. I even like the whole philosophy behind your lifestyle, and it has a lot of appeal. I just think being spanked for going to my flat is a bit much."

"I understand that, but it's not so much that you went to your flat and you don't think that was a dangerous thing to do. I disagree, but that, too, is not the point. Just because nothing happened doesn't mean that it couldn't have. But more importantly, you're going to accept my discipline because it's part of the whole agreement we're making. And regardless of how it turned out, you disobeyed me."

Rachel sat for a moment longer. He could practically see the wheels turning in her head as she listened to what he had to say. That was a good sign. He'd been right; she wasn't one to act impulsively, but rather tended to reason things out. It didn't mean that she wouldn't act out, but at least he would know she'd done it deliberately.

Without another word, she stood and marched herself into the bedroom. He could hear her removing her clothes—a delicious sound. He gave her a moment alone; he wanted her to really understand and accept what was about to happen. Afterwards, he would talk to her about it all, but right now, he needed to know she truly wanted to proceed and that she would accept his protection, his authority and his discipline. He also wanted her to accept the pleasure he could afford her. His cock grew hard just thinking about her orgasming at his touch.

Holmes stood and tried to adjust himself so his arousal wasn't painfully obvious. Yes, he wanted to have sex with her, but he wanted so much more from her as well. He wanted with Rachel what Roark had with Sage—the intimacy, the connection, the love.

When he entered the room, the sight that greeted him was one he hadn't expected. Rachel was naked, but she wasn't sitting on the edge of the bed as he'd instructed. Instead, she was kneeling in the middle of the bed. Her palms rested on her thighs, her eyes cast down, a submissive accepting her Dom's authority and waiting for her punishment. Clearly, she'd done some reading. He could tell by her posture that she was nervous, but that was to be expected. Her hair fell in soft waves down around her shoulders, tempting him to run his fingers through it.

Holmes groaned, his cock vying for control with his brain. He'd seen plenty of submissives kneeling in a similar position, waiting for what they knew would follow—pain and pleasure tied together in an intimate dance for supremacy. But there was something about Rachel offering herself that aroused him like nothing else ever had.

In the club, he'd seen and played with many subs and had seen them awaiting his dominance, kneeling on the floor. But although he was strict, he didn't like to think of himself as a hard top and was practical and worked to ensure his partner was comfortable before any scene started. Neither he nor Rachel were the proverbial spring chickens, and he imagined the bed was far kinder to older bones than the floor.

The idea that she had done some reading and was trying to please him did things for him that no other woman had done before—in real life or in the books Sage had written. And his dick was threatening to take over completely. If this moment of discipline was going to be effective, he was going to have to keep his focus. And he desperately wanted this to be effective. More than anything, he wanted to rid her of the malevolent presence that had attached itself to her. He needed to keep her safe so they could have a future together.

He'd been right about her figure that first time he'd seen her. She wore frumpy clothes to hide her lush figure. Given what had brought her to England, he could understand that decision. But for their relationship to work, she needed to accept that she had nothing to fear. She needed to embrace his showing her off—clothed and unclothed. The diaphanous nightgown last night only hinted at what lay beneath—a stunning body, tall, with long legs and large breasts. A small, well-defined waist that gave way to generous hips he could hold onto as he fucked her.

His brain made a last-ditch attempt to take over. He knew before he made love to her—and he was quickly beginning to accept that as inevitable—he should tell her the truth. But if she was going to reject him and run from him in horror, he wanted at least to have had this one moment with her.

Rachel looked up at him. "Is this all right? I know you said sitting, but the articles I read made a big deal about the kneeling part. They said the floor, but…"

He cupped her chin in his hand. "You're fine, sweetheart. You look lovely. I've never had a sub present herself in a way that stirred me the way you do. Your form is excellent, but you might want to straighten your back a bit and spread your legs wider."

She smiled, and her body lost a lot of the rigidity it had been holding as she adjusted her posture.

"As pretty as this picture is, you are owed discipline and I mean to see you get it," he said, suppressing a smile. The look on her crestfallen face was hard to resist. The internal struggle to keep from either laughing or kissing her was real, visceral, and difficult not to give into.

So that was what the kneeling was about—not truly accepting his authority but trying to seduce him out of a punishment. That wasn't going to work. He was made of sterner stuff than that. Rachel would find that topping from the bottom would never get her the result she wanted. He realized that theirs would be a different kind of relationship than that of Roark and Sage. There would be a power exchange between him and Rachel, but it would be more give and take —a kind of dance that left both of them breathless.

Sitting down on the bed, he patted his thigh. "Over my knee, Rachel."

He didn't think for even a second the slight hitch in her breath came from anything other than arousal. He inhaled deeply and caught the sweet fragrance of her desire. Rachel crawled over to him and slid across his lap as though she'd done it a thousand times before. Maybe she had. Maybe in another life, in another book, they had been lovers and were only now rediscovering each other in this existence.

She lay across his thighs, wriggling to find a comfortable spot. All the while his hard cock strained against his trousers and throbbed against her belly. There was no help for that, but at least she would have no question about whether he wanted her or not. He rubbed her backside with his right hand—she had skin like silk, and her flesh quivered beneath his touch. With the other, he steadied her and held her in place.

"Do you understand why you're being spanked?" he asked.

"Yes."

"Yes, Sir. When we're playing or you're being disciplined, I expect you to call me Sir. So, do you understand why I'm going to turn this gorgeous ass of yours bright red?"

"Yes, Sir. Because you told me to stay at the hotel and I didn't."

"That, and I told you if you disobeyed me, I would discipline you. I want you to know you can depend on me to do what I think is best for you, even if it isn't what I want to do in the moment."

"I'm fine with it if you don't want to." She tried to get up.

The sharp crack of his hand against her ass echoed through the room. He hadn't smacked her that hard, yet she yelped as her pale skin began to color. He doubted Rachel had ever been spanked in her life.

"I'm sure you would prefer that," he mused aloud. "But it's important you learn from the get-go that if you disobey me, you can expect to get disciplined, and that trying to manipulate me to get out of a punishment will only make it worse."

CHAPTER 10

Rachel couldn't believe she was actually going to do this. What was worse was how incredibly turned on the idea made her feel. She'd tried to tell herself it was just Holmes she was so attracted to, but that was a lie. The more she'd read this morning, the more curious and attracted to the lifestyle she'd become. The idea of being able to turn everything over to someone else so she could have a few moments when her mind was going a hundred miles an hour was seductive.

"Do you understand that this isn't like at the club? I don't just want to play with you, Rachel. I'd like this to be the start of something extraordinary."

"Yes, Sir. The way the contract is worded made it very clear, and you're right—it does make things easier knowing what each of us wants."

"I don't just want a sub in the bedroom. I want a

woman who submits to me and trusts that I will always put her needs first. That doesn't mean you'll always get what you want, but you will definitely get what you need."

The cool, recirculated, rarefied air of the Savoy's air-conditioning passed over her heated flesh. His cock pressed eagerly against her belly. He was hard… and big. She shivered again, as Holmes stroked her spine with one hand, his other resting on her butt cheek.

"You don't have to do this," he reminded her. "If at any time you want to opt out, all you have to do is use your safe word, and everything comes to a screeching halt."

"What if I just need a moment?" she asked.

"Some couples use the stoplight system—green means everything is good, yellow means you need a break but intend to go back to it, and red means stop. You said Tudor is your word for stop. You can use yellow and green or come up with words for those as well. Or you could just tell me you need a moment to gather yourself."

"I think right now I'd be the most comfortable with the last one."

"That'll work. Any other questions or concerns before I spank you?"

"Just one."

"What's that?" Was that a note of frustration she heard in his voice?

"Are we going to fuck afterwards?"

He chuckled. "I'd watch turning that bratty mouth on me, if I were you."

She had only the tiniest fraction of a moment between when his large hand lifted up off her backside before it came crashing down to consider what was about to happen. As it landed, the pain caused her whole body to light up in a way it never had. Was this what had been missing her whole life?

There was the briefest uptake in the air before his hand landed again on the other cheek. Pain flared, followed by a delicious heat that radiated out from where he'd struck. Rachel was surprised to feel tears welling up. The way pain and pleasure danced together was something she'd never felt before. Emotion flowed between her and Holmes without measure or resistance. Did he need to discipline her in the same way she suddenly seemed to need him to?

Once again, she noticed the swift disturbance in the air as his hand left her ass, only to come back down, sharply striking her bare flesh. The burn that spread out from where his hand landed felt sweet somehow, and it sparked the flame of desire she had long thought dead. Desire and need coursed through her body. Rachel moaned, maybe from the pain, or maybe from the arousal the spanking sent surging through her system. Perhaps both.

Over and over, he spanked her. At first, each time his hand connected with her bottom, her body tensed from the pain, but as he settled into a rhythm, her body knew what to expect and relaxed into it. Holmes laid into her. Apparently he wanted to ensure that she felt every blow and commit to memory the consequences for disobedience.

Rachel felt herself let go and just be—no past, no future, only the present. A blissful peace rapidly rivaled the pain and pleasure that heated her blood and raced through her veins. She began to understand what attracted so many strong, independent people to this lifestyle. She felt no worry here, just an understanding that she was not alone and there was someone who cared for her.

At first, she'd tried to keep count of how many times he spanked her, but soon let that go too. Tears began to leak out of her eyes, releasing the terror and strain she'd been living with since the entity had attached itself to her. Although she didn't cry out, the simple act of no longer holding in her tears or the fear that accompanied them was liberating. Everything that had gone before, everything she had pushed down into a little well of negativity, drained out of her body as she cried.

A kind of cleansing was taking place—clearing out that space where all the negative emotions and thoughts had resided to make room for something new. Something better. Rachel let the tears fall freely.

"That's my girl. Just let it go. I've got you," he crooned.

Finally, in a moment that felt as short as a heartbeat and as long as a cathartic eternity, his hand came to rest lightly on her overly sensitized flesh, holding its heat against her skin as if to keep it there forever. Whatever happened now or in the future, she knew she wouldn't regret the choice she'd made today—well, she might want to rethink disobeying him. Holmes had a wicked hand, and yet now that same hand imparted the softest caress where only moments before it had punished and chastised.

∽

Rachel had responded so well to his discipline. He'd known she would. She was a submissive at heart—an alpha submissive, one who would only submit to one man, but a submissive, nonetheless. At first her body had been tense, but it hadn't taken long before the tears had begun to fall and with them, the rigidity in her posture had given way to the softness of acceptance and trust. Her response had only made his cock that much harder.

He continued to soothe her well-colored backside, which was a glorious shade of red, letting his fingers slip between her legs to confirm what his nostrils told him. A smile came over his face. Rachel was soaking wet. As he grazed over the sensitive flesh, she moaned.

Holmes parted her labia and penetrated her cunt with two large fingers. Her abundant slickness ensured he had an easy entrance. He curled his fingers down to stroke the sweet spot that lay deep inside a woman's sheath. Rachel's breath hitched. He grinned further.

"It's all right, sweetheart," he assured her. "There's nothing wrong with having a spanking that lights up your body, readying it for mine. So in answer to your earlier question, yes, we're going to fuck. But first, you're going to use your mouth to pleasure me as a thank-you for my discipline."

He grabbed a pillow and tossed it down onto the floor at his feet. Holmes slid Rachel off his lap and down onto her knees between his legs. Unbuckling his belt, he opened his fly and freed himself. Her eyes widened, and she licked her lips.

"Suck my cock," he ordered.

As if they had been together for a long time and used to complying with his commands, she parted her lips just as he thrust his throbbing dick into her mouth. Her tongue swirled around his staff, and he groaned. There would come a time he would teach her exactly how he wanted her to service him, but for right now, just being in her mouth was torture enough.

Fisting her hair in his hands to hold her steady, he began to use her mouth in a way that would suffice until he shoved his cock deep inside her body and truly possessed her. Tonight, it would be her pussy, but he promised himself he would also have her ass.

"Deeper. Let me in, Rachel. Suck my cock."

Steadying her head, he watched as he drove his cock to the soft place at the back of her throat, forcing her to take his entire length in. Watching as it disappeared past her lips was almost his undoing. As he dragged his cock back, she sucked more deeply, trying to keep him inside. And she didn't just suck; her tongue laved his entire length, rolling over and around him.

There was a part of him that simply wanted to burrow deep in her mouth, spilling his cum down her throat. But he wanted more for him, for her, for them. He wasn't going to come the first time and not be buried in her soft, wet, ripe pussy. No way. He reluctantly withdrew from her mouth, his cock threatening to kill him. He soothed its ire by reminding it that as good as her mouth might be, there was nothing it enjoyed more than being buried balls deep in the wet heat of a woman's cunt. Nothing.

Holmes helped her to her feet and back onto the bed, arranging her on her back so that she was spread out for him like a feast. He would most likely have to fuck her from behind most of the time to keep her mindful that she was his sub, but he meant to make each and every time he had her unforgettable until he crowded out the memories of all she had known before.

He crawled up onto the bed, spreading her legs and pushing them apart. Rachel lay opened, vulnerable to him. The petals of her sex were soft and swollen with her need. He smelled her arousal and longed to bury his face in her, but that, too, would have to wait for another day. He meant to mount and fuck her. Hard.

He anticipated a lot of long, rainy afternoons and evenings in the future, spending his time seeing just how many times he could make her come. Some Doms liked to play at orgasm denial, but Holmes far preferred forced ones—leaving his sub spent and exhausted from what he did to her.

Like a heat-seeking missile, his cock zeroed in on its target, the ripe silo of her sheath. Slowly, he began to push his way in. He'd known she was going to be a tight fit, but the ecstasy of sinking into her for the first time felt exquisite beyond measure. Sighing in delight, Rachel tilted her hips to give him easier access. She didn't play coy, didn't try to hide what she was feeling. Her eyes locked with his and widened, darkening with pure lust as he tunneled his way in.

He pressed himself into her until he reached his hilt, his balls snug up against her. Heaven. He stilled for a moment, letting her body get used to being filled by him. She would have to adjust quickly because he intended to be inside her several times a day. He closed his eyes just for a moment to indulge in the sheer hedonistic pleasure of having her pussy pulsing in time to the throbbing of his cock.

Perfect synchronicity.

Opening his eyes, he pulled himself back and then

thrust into her, hard and fast. Her pussy seemed to be sucking at his dick to keep it inside. It didn't want to let go. That was good, because he wasn't going anywhere. In that moment, he was glad the spanking had so primed her for his possession, because he wasn't going to be able to fuck her for hours like he wanted to. No, this first time he would ensure she climaxed, but then he was going to have to come.

"Mine," he growled.

"Yes," she purred.

Holmes pounded into her, ruthless in his need to dominate and conquer. Arching her body, Rachel cried out as she came. Her orgasm was so powerful, it washed over them both. Her pussy clamped down hard and he smiled. If she was that easy, she was going to spend a lot of the rest of her life sore from his use. Watching her come was an intense combination of feelings—affection and lust, tender and possessive. Never had a woman seemed to fit him like Rachel. She was the one thing Sage hadn't provided for him in her books.

The tingle at the base of his spine signaled he didn't have much more time to revel in her singular acceptance of all he had to offer her. Holmes thrust in and out of her in a faster, stronger rhythm, ensuring he hit her G-spot on at least every other stroke. He was determined he would make her come again as he emptied himself into her.

Over and over, he hammered her pussy with a

savage need he had never felt before. Calling his name, Rachel came a second time as he began to spill himself in her. He ground himself against her as her pussy milked his cock, contracting up and down his length, ensuring he had nothing left to give her.

When at last he was done, he collapsed on top of her for a moment, allowing her to take his weight before easing himself from her body and rolling onto his back. He drew her up gently alongside him.

CHAPTER 11

Rachel didn't remember when she'd fallen asleep. But when she woke, it seemed as though the light was softening as it did when day began to wane and give over to the moonlight. Her most feminine parts ached, both from Holmes' size and the two times he had fucked her. The first had been an exquisite revelation, but the second had made the first pale in comparison. As she rolled onto her backside, she was reminded of the discipline he'd inflicted before making love to her.

He wasn't in bed next to her. It sounded as if he was in the other room, answering the door and letting room service in. Good; she was hungry. Holmes rolled the trolley into the bedroom—even better.

Stopping at the foot of the bed, he came forward, took her face in his hands and kissed her deeply and thoroughly. When he'd finished, she was breathless. Desire began to hum through her body again.

"Are you all right?" he asked.

"Better than I've been in a very long time. I don't suppose I could persuade you to come back to bed, could I?"

"Tempting, but we've got work to do. I had something brought up for us to snack on, as I doubt you stopped to get anything to eat earlier. And if your fridge yesterday was any indication, it isn't just sleep you've been missing." He arched an eyebrow.

She was quiet for a moment. "No, Sir," she admitted. "I was intent on getting to my flat, getting what I needed and getting back here."

"Hoping you could do so before I returned?"

"Yes, but I would have told you because, as you like to point out to me, you're a detective with Scotland Yard. I'm pretty sure you would have noticed the extra laptop and clothes. Also, I really did take to heart what you said yesterday about not being completely honest with you, and honestly lies at the heart of D/s. I hope you aren't still angry with me that I left the hotel."

"Not at all. That's another advantage of D/s—if there's a problem, you deal with it and then it's done. You disobeyed me, you got punished and the slate is wiped clean. Do me a favor?"

"Anything," she said, realizing she meant it.

"Put something on, and let's eat in the other

room."

"What's the matter, Holmes?" she said, slithering off the bed seductively and circling him, rubbing her body all along his as she did so, smiling as she faced him and was confronted by his hard cock.

Holmes smacked her already aching backside. "Not appropriate. It's perfectly fine to tell me you'd like to have sex, or anything else for that matter. But the next time you think to play the cock-tease with me, I'll put you in four-point restraints and make you suck me off several times a day while I play with you, keeping you on edge until I think you've learned your lesson."

She searched his face and realized he wasn't angry or trying to be intimidating; he was just giving her the information he thought she needed to make the right decision. She backed off, casting her eyes down. He lifted her chin up. "I'm not angry at you. I know this is all new to you. You just need to know that spanking you is probably the form of discipline you'll prefer. I can be a mean and nasty Dom when I'm pissed, but I will never hurt you. At least not in a way you won't ultimately like. Understand?"

She nodded. "Yes, and thanks for understanding that reading and practicing are two entirely different things. But can I ask you something?"

"Always."

"Can I flirt with you?"

"Absolutely, and I'm flattered you think I'm worth

the effort. But there's a difference between flirting with me and teasing me to get your way. One I'll thoroughly enjoy, the other will earn you a punishment you will not appreciate."

"Yes, Sir. One last thing. I thought you said I'd be spending a lot of time naked if I signed that contract. Was I not what you…?" Rachel stopped, unsure of how to finish the sentence. She really didn't have any body image issues. But at forty years old, she didn't have the physique of a nineteen-year-old virgin—and there was always that last ten pounds she promised herself she'd lose.

"Finish that thought, much less that sentence, and I'll have you back over my knee so fast, it'll make your head spin. For the record, you are the single most gorgeous thing I've ever seen in my life. When I die, my only regret will be that we haven't had enough time together. I'm sure it's far too early to say this, but I love you, Rachel."

She stepped back from him as if he'd slapped her.

He inhaled deeply. "You don't have to say…"

Rachel flung herself into his arms, kissing him with a wild, abandoned passion that until this afternoon she hadn't known she was capable of. "I love you too. I was afraid I was fooling myself or that we'd only be together for however long it takes to get rid of this thing that's haunting me. But then I found myself wanting it to take forever. Pretty sick, huh?"

Holmes picked her up, holding her firmly up so

that her legs wrapped around his waist, and she was looking down at him. "If that's sick," he said, "let's pray they never find the cure."

Setting her back on the ground, he kissed her, a mere brush of his lips that left her senses reeling. "Get dressed and join me in the other room. I want to talk to you about what we observed and what you know about the Ripper murders."

She laughed. "From I love you to gruesome killings. I guess that's life with a DSI. Do you mean 'clothes' clothes, or can I just slip on your shirt? I really like the way that felt."

He grinned. "The shirt would be fine and practical. That way when I'm done talking about supernatural phenomenon and how to destroy it, I can just toss you on your back and fuck you silly."

Rachel laughed again, admiring the way his trousers emphasized his gorgeous butt as he left the room. She slipped on his shirt and joined him.

∽

She loved him. She said she did, and Holmes doubted she'd have said it just to be polite. More surprisingly, he'd said it first—something he'd never done before. Sage had never written his character to have any emotional involvement with the women he fucked, so Rachel had the distinction of being the first and only woman he'd ever said those words to. He wanted her to be the last. But now that he'd said it, the unspoken truth that lay between them seemed to be an almost insurmountable obstacle.

He wanted to tell himself it was because he worried that she'd tell their secret—his, Roark's and Felix's. But that wasn't it, and he damn well knew it. He didn't believe for even a second Rachel would do anything to harm or betray them. But he worried she would be afraid, especially with this thing stalking her. What if she saw him and that creature as the same kind of thing?

Roark was right. She deserved to know. Holmes would tell her, but he wanted to bind her to him first, in as many ways as he could—sex, protection, dominance, love. The question was, would she believe he loved her at all when he told her? Or would she see the other three for the manipulations he knew them to be? But if he did it right, and she was bound to him, they'd have a relationship well founded in all four. As her Dom, he'd tell her to listen, and she would.

He shook his head. No, that argument would never fly. He'd have to figure out how to tell her and not lose her.

Rachel came up behind him, wrapping her arms around him as she pressed herself against his back. "Are we insane?" she whispered.

He turned within her embrace and held her close. "Because we're chasing something not from this world?"

"Well, that too, I guess, but I was talking about falling in love with someone I haven't even known for forty-eight hours."

"If you are, so am I. But I think time is just part of the equation. When everything else falls into place, time is irrelevant."

"I guess that's true enough," she said as he sat down and drew her into his lap.

Holmes had ordered up a selection of appetizers, and they smelled delicious—decadent duck sliders on a bao bun with hoisin, arancini with truffles and mozzarella, brie in puff pastry and root vegetable crisps with romesco sauce. He dipped one of the crisps into the sauce, holding it up to her lips. She took the bite, sucking the dip from his fingers. She closed her eyes and sighed. The taste had exceeded the aroma. Holmes enjoyed having Rachel in his lap feeding her. She might well have to get used to having all her meals not eaten with others, sitting in his lap.

"Sage ate something with her publisher earlier, but Roark invited us to join them for dinner."

"I know you told me not to worry about the expense…"

"And you don't need to. I was born into family money that my father invested very well. He also made money on his own so when they died, my parents left me with a mortgage-free house in Chelsea and a substantial inheritance. I sold my flat and added that money to my nest egg. In all honesty, I could easily live off my salary from the Yard, so money is not something you need to worry about."

"For what it's worth, I've been able to make a comfortable living with my tours. What part of Chelsea?"

He grinned. "A brick row home overlooking the Thames—cobblestone street and a nice-sized back garden. It's lovely, but if you'd rather have something different or that we got together..."

"No. I think it sounds amazing. But can't we go there until after whatever it is with this thing is over? I thought about it when I went back to my flat this morning; I don't want to live somewhere it's been."

"So Mary Kelly's room is out?" he quipped. "I do understand, and I think you'll love the Chelsea house, but if you don't, we'll sell it and find some place you do. Do you own or rent your flat?"

"Own. I want to make sure that thing is gone not just from me but from the flat before we decide what we want to do with it." He smiled. "What?"

"I like how you already think in terms of we and our."

She laughed and relaxed against him. "Me too. So, you think it's connected to her—to him?"

"Don't you?"

"I hate to admit it, but yes. When you and Roark went there this morning, were you already thinking that?"

"It was too coincidental to think otherwise.

Besides, both Roark and I saw whatever it is last night as it came through the balcony door."

"Watson thought I made it up to boost my tour sales."

"He what?" growled Holmes.

"Don't go into over-protective mode. He had a legitimate concern, and he discussed it with me. He doesn't believe that now. I think he and I will be good friends."

"He had no right…"

"Of course he did. He's your friend and he barely knew me. So tell me what happened."

She settled into his lap as if he was going to tell her her favorite bedtime story, a behavior he found charming. "Mrs. McCarthy met us to let us in. The room struck me as to how unassuming it was. How very mundane and normal. She opened the door and sort of stood back."

Rachel nodded. "Yes, she doesn't like going in there."

"After having visited today, I understand why. There was a noticeable drop in the temperature, and it just felt odd. And Roark and I know odd." He picked up one of the duck sliders, dipping it in the sauce and saying, "Here, try this. I think they're my favorites."

As she sucked on his fingers he wondered if she knew how that affected his dick, which had become painfully aroused. He saw the smile on her face—yeah, she knew.

"How so?" she asked.

Covering quickly, he said, "Both of us have been in law enforcement, detective work and a bit of the spy game for years. Things are rarely what they seem. But after last night and seeing—or not seeing—whatever was there, we certainly couldn't help but know we are dealing with something not of this world."

"I'm sorry if seeing that thing threw the two of you, but honestly, just knowing someone else could see and feel it was inordinately comforting. I mean, I trusted my eyes, but I did have moments when I questioned my own sanity." She snuggled into him, nuzzling his neck and relaxing completely.

Holding her close, he said, "No, sweetheart, there is something there and it has attached itself to you. Mrs. McCarthy explained that the owners had taken the pictures of the crime scene and recreated the room's contents as best they could. The only thing left that is original is the big mirror bolted over the fireplace."

"Gorgeous old thing, but sometimes I get the feeling that it's watching me—kind of like those pictures where it looks like the eyes are following you around the room. It has always been creepy and given me the willies. The Ripper tour is one of the few I don't look forward to taking clients on."

"Mrs. McCarthy said the same thing. She said she

sometimes felt like something was watching her from the other side of the mirror. When you were there, did the mirror have a crack in it?"

"A crack? No. It was in perfect shape. It's not the best reflective quality since it's only polished obsidian, not glass. But no, there was nothing wrong with it."

"There is now. There's a large crack running up the center. I swabbed it and had a friend at the Yard's forensics lab run a trace analysis. He was curious so did it himself and got back to me with the preliminary results. He wants to do some further analysis."

"What did he find?" she asked, offering him the last bite of the puffed pasty filled with brie.

"Nothing human, but he did find nucleotides which apparently…"

"Combine to form DNA," she whispered. "Anything else?"

"Yes, something called dark matter."

The color drained from Rachel's face and her body trembled as the import of what the lab results indicated. She looked at him. He knew she wanted him to give her any explanation other than the obvious one, but he shook his head, dashing her hopes for some other more rational reason. He wouldn't lie to her to keep her from being afraid, but he could and would keep her safe. Whatever the hell this thing was, it was going back and leaving his woman alone.

"Holmes, do you think somehow Jack the Ripper has come back through the mirror?"

CHAPTER 12

She'd come to the same conclusion he had. Ever since he'd talked to the lab, he'd tried to wrap his mind around what it could mean, grasping at anything that didn't lead back to the idea that somehow Jack the Ripper was trying to make his way back into the world. What he didn't know, and that he needed to tell Rachel, was that he wasn't just a DSI with Scotland Yard. The Ripper would be facing off with a group of men who understood paranormal phenomenon better than most, as they themselves were of supernatural origin.

He'd wondered how he would ever come up with a way to introduce her to the idea of who and what he was. It seemed the time had come. Would he have the courage to tell her? What if she didn't believe him? What if she did? Would finding herself involved with a man not born of this world terrify her the way the malevolent apparition did?

"What was it my fictional ancestor was supposed to have said? *When you've eliminated the impossible, you're left with the improbable as the truth.* I don't want to think that's true, but…"

"It would explain why he was never heard from again after Mary Kelly's death."

"Didn't they try to pin other murders on him?"

Rachel nodded. "Yes, both in Europe and in America. But if we accept that the Ripper is in some form back among us, how did it happen? Will he start killing again? How do we send him back and make sure he never escapes again?"

"Unknown. For me, the second question is the most pressing and has a follow-up—are you his intended first victim?"

"One of the things they believe about the Ripper is that he hated women. And that thing, if it is the Ripper, did call me a whore last night."

"It did. I don't like the fact that it seems to have attached itself to you, but the question is why you?"

"I have no idea. It doesn't help that there is very little known about the Ripper or most of his victims. We know more about them in death than we do of their lives, especially Mary Kelly."

"Yes. Her life seems fairly tragic."

"I think a lot of women led fairly tragic lives back then. One thing all the accounts say was that she was a nice woman. There are stories that she offered a safe sleeping place to other prostitutes who couldn't even afford a shabby room. If we assume the Ripper has come back from the dead, how did he do it? Where was he all this time?"

And there it was again—the proverbial elephant in the room. Although he hadn't come back from the dead, he knew more about piercing the veil and coming through than most people. He and Felix had always felt like they stumbled through. They had not been fully sentient until they'd found themselves outside the pages of Sage's books. Actually, it was Roark who knew the most, as he had come through the veil in order to save Sage.

"What do you know about the veil between the two worlds?" he asked.

"Actually, more than you might think. I had a roommate my first year in college who was a practicing pagan, and I minored in Irish mythology."

That surprised him. Rachel had always—although always was a relative term—struck him as highly practical. Part of his reluctance to tell her about his existence and how he came to be was that she wouldn't believe him or be able to accept who and what he was. *Liar*, whispered his conscience. His reluctance stemmed from one thing and one thing only. Fear. Somehow, inexplicably, he had fallen head-over-heels in love with Rachel, and the thought of life without her was unbearable.

"The veil," she continued, slipping into quasi-professorial mode, "is said to separate the mundane, material world in which we live from the spiritual world on the other side."

"Do you believe in another side?" he asked.

"I don't see how you can't. I know of no culture that doesn't believe in something beyond death. They may all believe different things and call it different names, but when so many disparate people have a common belief, there must be something to it."

"Do you think that those of us on this side can communicate with those on the other?"

"That's a far more difficult thing to answer. I'm not sure, but I'd like to believe so. I do know that at certain times of the year, the veil is said to be more permeable than others. But many believe that with the right combination of forces, either side can penetrate the veil and travel between worlds."

"Like a revolving door?"

"No. Generally people see it as a one-way trip but going through to the other side and returning from where you started isn't unheard of."

Holmes considered her answer and then asked, "Can someone or something be pushed through the veil against its will?"

She nodded. "When I was studying the Irish myths, there were some beliefs around magick users being able to do that by casting a spell or cursing them. My favorite of those stories was the one that talked about calling the banshees to drag the person across the veil."

"I thought banshees were just the harbingers of death."

"That's the most common belief; others believe each of the great families have their own banshee that tries to protect that family. I came across one myth that they can be summoned to fight evil and drag it into the otherworld."

"So, there is a historical reference to being able to send this thing back to hell."

"There's no empirical evidence to prove that—just stories told by an ancient people to explain things they couldn't."

Holmes held her close. "I don't know that it's limited to ancient people. I think we still do that today. Things we don't understand, we try to explain in a way that makes sense. For instance, there is no empirical evidence that there is something stalking you, but we saw it. We heard it. We know it was there."

"I suppose that's true," she said.

"Wasn't Mary Kelly from Ireland?"

"Yes. It's one of the few things everyone agrees on. Some of her neighbors were frightened of her, and it's said her cousin forced her from the cousin's home. There are two versions to that story. The first, and most widely accepted, is that Mary became a prostitute, and her cousin didn't approve."

"What's the other theory?"

Rachel smiled and wiggled her fingers in front of him, humming the theme from *The Twilight Zone*. "That Mary was a powerful witch. Those who subscribe to that theory believe that not only was her cousin frightened by the power Mary could wield, but that the authorities would take a dim view of a witch living in Cardiff."

"They weren't burning witches during Victoria's reign."

"Not officially, but the church still held sway during that time. It's not inconceivable that her cousin was afraid of being ostracized or shunned by her community. But if the Ripper is back, why is he attached to me?"

"Did you hear the mirror crack when you were at the door? Maybe you were the closest human when it escaped."

"I didn't hear anything like that, but I did hear what sounded like a terrified man's scream. If Mary Kelly somehow reached beyond her death to curse him into the mirror, even someone like the Ripper might have cried out. Maybe I was hearing some kind of psychic reverberation from his last moments on this side of the veil. If that is what happened the night Mary Kelly died, then it makes some sense that it would latch on to the first living being it encountered."

"The thing that bothers me the most is that it seems to be gaining strength. You said last night was the first time it spoke."

She nodded. "The other thing I noticed was that it seems to be gaining some kind of shape. It's losing more and more of its translucent quality. Last night, it bordered on being opaque."

"I don't suppose your studies included a guide to getting rid of an unwanted ghost."

"Not ghost," corrected Rachel. "A spirit."

"Is there a difference?"

"Most think of a ghost as having a human shape and recognizable features. A spirit is kind of like a disembodied ghost—no real shape, hard to see. And I don't have a how-to guide, but I may know someone who can answer some questions."

"Who?" he asked suspiciously.

"My old roommate. If she doesn't know firsthand, she will know who to ask." She reached for her mobile phone, which was laying on the coffee table.

"We're supposed to meet Roark and Sage for dinner in an hour or so. Do you have time to call her before then?"

"I think so." Rachel scrolled through her contacts and dialed her old friend, putting the call on speaker phone. "Saoirse? It's Rachel Moriarty."

"Rachel," a feminine voice with the heavy Irish accent answered. "It's so good to hear from you. Are you still planning that tour of Ireland?"

"I am. The clients say probably late summer, early fall of next year. They really want to stay off the beaten path, but that's not what I'm calling about. Do you have time to talk?"

"For you, always. What's up?"

"I have you on speaker phone, and I have a detective with Scotland Yard here with me."

"The Yard? What the hell are you involved with?"

"Something weird."

"So naturally you called me. Thanks, I think," said Saoirse. "Before we go any further, tell me about the detective. Is he cute?"

"Very," laughed Rachel. "Kind of stupid gorgeous, lots of rippling muscles."

"How's he hung?"

"That's enough," growled Holmes.

"That small?" teased Saoirse.

"No," smiled Rachel, "that big and he knows what to do with it."

"Rachel, what part of that's enough did you not understand?" said Holmes, arching his eyebrow at her.

"Oooh, and he sounds like a Dom."

"He is," agreed Rachel, "so don't get me in trouble."

"As I recall, we had quite a lot of fun getting in trouble back in the day. But you didn't call to reminisce. How can I help?"

"Do you know much about Jack the Ripper and his final victim?"

"Aye. Mary Kelly—she was Irish, born in Limerick if I recall."

"A little more than a week ago, I was giving a tour of the murder sites."

"I've warned you to stay away from those places. No one ever found him," said Saoirse. "There's many of us in the magickal community of Ireland who think somehow Mary Kelly found a way to get him."

"But there wasn't a body," said Holmes.

"And there wouldn't be if she spell-cast him and cursed him into an object. Why are you asking?"

"Here's the weird part. I realized the door had come open to Mary's room. When I went to close it, something pushed it shut from the other side. I heard a scream…"

"A man's scream?"

"Yes, and then it felt like a gust of wind push through me."

"Does your copper with the cock believe in the supernatural?" said Saoirse, sarcastically and with a verbal nod towards Holmes.

"I can't help but believe. I've seen the thing," he answered.

"Damn. Was there a mirror in that room opposite the door?" asked Saoirse.

"Yes. It hung over the fireplace," said Rachel. "Some descriptions of the scene say it was a picture, but it wasn't."

"The caretaker said it was the only piece that wasn't

a reproduction. Mrs. McCarthy said it gave her the creeps, and sometimes she felt there was something on the other side looking back at her," explained Holmes.

"What was the mirror made of?" asked Saoirse in a hushed voice.

"The same things most mirrors of the time were made of, polished obsidian," answered Rachel. "Is that important?"

"It is. Obsidian is a powerful stone that protects. If Mary Kelly had the knowledge and power, she might have been able to delay her departure from one realm to the next in order to cast him into the mirror. The obsidian would be able to hold his evil on the other side of the veil."

"And if the mirror cracked?" asked Holmes, afraid he knew the answer.

"Then whatever had been cast or cursed into the mirror would have a chance to escape, but only if it could find a human tether on the other side. You say you've seen it?"

"Yes. It's what sent me to Scotland Yard. I didn't know the mirror had cracked, but ever since I felt that gust of wind, I haven't been able to sleep. The thing unlocks my door from the outside and comes toward me."

"Has the apparition changed?"

"Yes. Both in appearance and demeanor."

"How so?"

"At first I could easily see through it. The only way I knew there was something was a vague blurred shape. It has gotten more defined and more opaque. And it's become more assertive."

"I'd call it aggressive," said Holmes. "Last night it called her a whore."

"You need to leave your flat," said Saoirse.

"I did."

"You shouldn't be alone. Does it show up at the same time?"

"Generally between two and four in the morning."

"Damn. The witching hour. It's learned."

"Do you think this thing is sentient?" asked Holmes.

"I'd bet on it," said Saoirse. "And that's the only time you see it?"

"Yes," answered Rachel. "Is that important? I know all of the Ripper murders happened between one and five in the morning."

"It's gathering strength. If it comes at you during the witching hour, it takes the least amount of effort. And you've left your flat. But it's still coming. You shouldn't be alone."

"I'm not. I'm staying at the Savoy with Holmes. Both he and his friend Roark Samuels, the detective, have seen it."

"Did you call your copper Holmes?"

"Yes. Michael Holmes. He's a DSI with Scotland Yard."

"That he is," said Saoirse. "I talked extensively several months ago with Samuels and his wife Sage. I know who and what you are, Holmes. Does Rachel?"

CHAPTER 13

"What does she mean?" asked Rachel, looking at him.

Her eyes were still guileless and full of trust. Holmes had told himself if he bound her to him with sex and affection and love, then maybe, just maybe, she would forgive him the lie of his emergence into this world.

"Hang up, Rachel."

"I don't understand."

"I know you don't. Hang up, Rachel, now."

As she ended the call, she slid off his lap before he'd even realized she was going to move. He closed his eyes. He had to figure a way out of this. He loved her. He could honestly tell her he'd never love another woman, and it was true. Of course, before last year he'd only existed in the pages of Sage Matthews' series of novels about a fictional *Bond-esque* detective named Roark Samuels.

Roark's, his and Felix's characters had all emerged from Sage's books last year when Sage had been in danger and Roark had pushed through the veil to save her.

How the hell was he going to explain this to her and not have her run screaming from the room? He loved her. He had no doubt about that; he was pretty damn sure she felt the same way. He couldn't keep withholding the entire truth from her. Hadn't he disciplined her for that very reason—not telling him the complete truth? Didn't that make him something of a hypocrite?

Holmes told himself his excuse was that he wanted to wait until Rachel was free of the apparition that had attached itself to her, threatening her. He wanted to keep her safe. But how did he justify that while continuing to lie to her? Hadn't he stressed that D/s was all about honesty and truth? How could he not tell her? He knew he couldn't continue to do so. He loved her.

"What's she talking about, Holmes?"

He could feel fear rolling off her, knowing it wasn't her physical safety that concerned her. Maybe it would be easier on her if he got Roark and Sage. He used the house phone to dial their room.

"I thought we were meeting in an hour or so," answered Roark without preamble.

"We have information on the apparition. We got it from an Irish woman named Saoirse," said Holmes.

"We're on our way," said Roark, hanging up the phone.

"Why did you call Roark? What is Saoirse talking about?"

"I can explain, sweetheart," he said, squeezing her hand and smiling in reassurance.

"Explain what?" she demanded, her voice taking on an edge.

Time to exert a little control before she got out of hand. "That's enough, Rachel. Watch your tone."

"Watch my tone? Are you fucking kidding me?" she snarled.

That was his Rachel—going from purring kitten to spitting wildcat in the space of a heartbeat. Just then, there came a discreet knock. Holmes answered the door, ushering Roark and Sage into the room.

Rachel whirled on Sage. "We were just talking to my college roommate, Saoirse. She says she met you last year, and you told her something very important about Roark and Holmes. What exactly did she know that I don't?" she demanded.

Instead of responding, Sage looked at her husband. "Roark, darling, why don't you make us all a cocktail? I think we're going to need them."

Rachel faced Sage head on. "I asked you a question, Sage. I would appreciate an honest answer. Saoirse seemed to think she knew something about

Roark and Holmes that I should know, especially as I was fucking Holmes."

Suddenly, Rachel looked down, as if she'd only now realized she was wearing nothing but his shirt. "Excuse me," she said, stalking back into the bedroom, shutting the door firmly behind her.

"What happened?" asked a concerned Sage.

"I warned you that you needed to tell her," said Roark as he mixed the drinks.

Holmes sighed and sat down, feeling utterly defeated. Before he could answer Roark, Rachel walked back in, wheeling her suitcase behind her and focusing her eyes anywhere but at him. "You know, it doesn't matter what Saoirse knows about you. I may have been stupid and vulnerable enough to believe you when you told me you had feelings for me…"

"I didn't say I had feelings for you, Rachel. I told you I loved you. And I have never said that to another woman. Sage can verify that."

Sage nodded at Rachel. "He's right. He's never been in love before." She turned to Holmes. "I'm so happy for you."

"Don't be. He can take his love and shove it up his ass. It isn't what he didn't tell me, it's the fact that there was anything to tell. I'll go back to Ireland, to Saoirse and see if she can't help me. I should have gone there in the first place."

Quietly wringing her hands, Sage glanced nervously back and forth between them.

Holmes shook his head and stood up. "You're not going anywhere without me. You're my woman, and I will bloody well protect you from whatever the hell this thing is. If you want to put our relationship on hold…"

"We don't have a relationship, Holmes. We had sex. Good sex, I'll grant you, but that's all it was," she said, the anger, hurt and disappointment evident on her face and in her voice.

Holmes clenched his fists, trying to control his own hurt and anger. "It was a hell of a lot more than that, and you know it."

He closed the space between them. Dragging her into his arms, fisting her hair and tugging on it to pull her head back before crushing his lips against hers. His other hand slipped from her waist down to her ass, grasping it and molding her lower body into his. He could feel his cock harden and poke at her belly as his tongue invaded and conquered her mouth.

Only vaguely and peripherally could he hear Sage say, "Roark?"

"Stay out of it, Sage. You don't come between a Dom and his sub. You know better, or do you need a refresher course on the breaking of that particular rule?"

God, he wanted what they had. He wanted it with every fiber of his being, and he meant to have it. He would not let her fear and anger drive them apart. Rachel had every right to be angry—he should have told her before now, but how could she deny what lay between them? He meant to make sure she couldn't. If she needed him to grovel, atone and make amends, he would. He would do whatever she needed to get them back where they had been before.

Rachel remained stiff and resistant only for a moment before giving over to the passion that flowed between them. Roark was right; he should have found a way to tell her, but he hadn't. He would make her understand; make her accept. But he also needed to remind her who was dominant and who was not. Rachel moaned into his mouth, her arms winding around his neck.

When he finally lifted his head, she slammed her knee into his groin, sending his nuts back up inside his body, and then stomped on his instep. She reached for her suitcase. Pain washed over him like a tidal wave. It was a good thing he'd never wanted to have children as he was pretty sure she'd done enough damage to ensure he couldn't sire any.

How the fuck had someone that beautiful, that much smaller than him, managed to cause him that much pain? It wasn't helping that he'd been aroused. What if she'd damaged him permanently? Well, she'd be as unhappy about that as he would be. The perverse part was, he was getting even harder. She was definitely going to be paying for causing not only the pain from her knee but from the resulting reaction he was having.

If he could move and if Sage and Roark weren't here, he'd likely throw her down, have her on her back and be shoving his battered and bruised cock up into her soft, wet pussy. Yes. That was the ticket. His cock needed to be enclosed in something warm, wet and female.

"Stop her," Holmes managed to grind out.

"Of course," said Roark, leaning back against the only exit out of the room. "Sweetheart," he said to Sage, "the cocktails will have to wait but see if you can't get Holmes some ice. That looked like it hurt."

"It did," said Holmes, trying to force air back into his lungs.

"Good," Rachel spat at him before turning to Roark. "Get out of my way or I'll..."

"You'll what?" asked Roark. The man's voice was deceptively calm, but Holmes knew him well enough to hear the sharp steel beneath it.

He had to get this situation under control, and fast. Rachel wasn't just threatening his existence or even Roark's. Though she didn't know it, she was threatening Sage's well-being too now, and that was something Roark would never allow.

"Rachel, that's enough," he insisted. "I'm willing to give you a pass on your behavior of the past few minutes because I realize you are upset—and rightly so. Something is threatening you, and the man you love who said he would protect you hasn't told you everything."

"Sauce for the goose…" Rachel started.

"But if you don't settle down right now and sit your ass on the couch, I will toss you over my knee and rain hellfire down on your ass. If you think the spanking I gave you earlier was bad, you will come to find out just how much I held back because it was your first time. Obey me, Rachel. Now."

Her shoulders sagged, deflated, like a balloon pricked by a pin. Tears welled in her eyes, but she headed to the other end of the sofa. Sage came back with an ice pack and shoved it against Holmes' crotch before sitting down next to Rachel to act as a barrier between them. Holmes looked to Roark, over to Sage, and back again.

"Sage, you know better than to interfere with a Dom and his sub. Come sit in the chair, and I'll make those cocktails if Holmes thinks he can guard the door."

"You're perfectly safe, Rachel. Holmes won't harm you," soothed Sage.

"I bloody well will if she tries a stunt like that again," growled Holmes.

"You lied to me," she whispered.

The sound of disappointment—no, disillusionment—cut him like a knife to the gut. Knowing there was no going forward without accepting what he'd done and telling her everything, he sat down on the sofa, giving her space.

"What does Saoirse know that I don't?" asked Rachel in as bleak a voice as he'd ever heard.

"I… that is to say we, being myself, Roark and Felix, are not of this world. Not exactly."

"You married some kind of demon?" Rachel asked Sage.

Sage laughed. "Not at all. Just your average, run-of-the-mill Neanderthal."

"Not helping, Sage," said Holmes, despondently. "Sweetheart, this is really difficult for me…"

"You'll forgive me if I'm not feeling terribly sorry for you." Truly in a temper now, Rachel looked so gorgeous when angry, and yet so remote too, it made the icy tendrils of fear wrap around his heart and squeeze.

Not seeing any easy entry into this difficult conversation, he sighed, moved closer to her and took her hands in his. When she moved to draw back, he held fast.

"Please, Rachel. If this is the last time you ever let me touch you, just let me hold your hands." She said nothing but ceased trying to pull away. "I fucked up. I lied to you. You have every reason in the world to be angry and not trust me. But I swear it wasn't intentional or planned. I didn't expect to fall in love with you. Did I have fantasies when we were at the Yard? Of course, I'm male; we're like that. But as I came to know you, I fell for you."

"What did you mean, not of this world?"

"Have you read Sage's Clive Thomas novels?" She nodded. "Up until about a year ago, they featured another detective, Roark Samuels, and his comrades."

"That's not true," Rachel said, looking at Sage.

"I'm afraid it is," said Roark's wife. "Well, actually, I'm not. If it weren't for Roark, I'd be dead. My publisher was embezzling funds from me and tried to kill me. But the books used to have different characters in the roles of Clive, his friend at the Yard, and the head concierge at the Savoy."

"How… how did it happen?"

Holmes shook his head as he rubbed his thumbs over the backs of her hands. "We don't know. Roark pushed through the veil to get to Sage. Felix and I just sort of woke up one day, and we were here. I had only been sentient and aware I was in the book for a very short time. Roark had been aware for a while before he broke through."

"Do you know he used to push past the veil, invade my dreams and have his way with me?" Sage added, her eyes dancing with amusement. "I used to have the most incredibly erotic dreams. Come to find out, my dream lover was my character and the love of my life. Some people talk about book boyfriends. I did 'em one better and have a book husband, who is also my Dom."

"But how?" persisted Rachel.

"None of us knows," said Holmes gently, moving closer to her.

"He's not holding back, Rachel. We don't know and only the five of us, and you make six, know anything about it. Holmes and Felix came through first. After I met them, I looked in the books and they'd been replaced."

"How frightening," Rachel said, glancing between Roark and Holmes, her face clouded with confusion, but some of the anger beginning to recede. She was a bit like a summer storm, erupting in a temper but fading away, leaving nothing but beauty and peace.

"At first, I thought it was somebody's idea of a joke. It's all rather fantastical. And even though I don't know how it happened, I'm glad it did." Sage looked up at Roark, her expression full of love and desire.

"You should have told me," said Rachel, stoically clinging to her anger and accusing Holmes of betrayal.

"Yes, I should," Holmes admitted. "And before you get angry at Roark or Sage, Roark berated me for not telling you yesterday morning, and I suspect Sage was none too pleased with my choice not to tell you."

"Why? I mean, I was already experiencing supernatural shit."

"Language, Rachel," Holmes said automatically. "I'm sorry. That was uncalled for. You're entitled to be angry and hurt and lash out at me in any way that will make you feel better. My only defense was that I was afraid if you knew, especially given what you were experiencing, you'd walk out of my life. I should have had more faith in you—more faith in us."

Rachel withdrew her hands from his, and he let her go. He'd lost her. He knew he would love her until the end of his days and damned his own lack of courage.

"I'd like to be by myself. I need to think."

"I understand," he said.

"But I can't afford to be by myself. Saoirse said this thing is dangerous. She probably has more to tell us, so we can call her back in the morning. I can't face this thing alone, and I'm pretty damn sure I can't beat it alone. Maybe you're the only people who can help me."

"I'll take care of you, Rachel. It'll have to kill me before it harms you in any way, shape or form. Why don't we order up some food? Or if you like, we can go downstairs. But we'll play this however you like."

Rachel stood and walked back to the bedroom, wheeling her suitcase behind her. In the doorway, she paused and looked at him. "That's the problem, Holmes; I wasn't playing."

CHAPTER 14

*R*achel closed the door behind her and leaned against it, letting the tears slide down her cheeks. He'd lied to her, and not just about something unimportant. He'd lied to her about the core of who he was. He wasn't human, nor were Roark or Felix. They had come from that same dark place as the creature that was after her. How could she know they weren't a part of it?

There was a light tapping on the door. "Rachel? It's Sage. Can I come in for just a minute?"

Rachel eased away from the door and opened it, allowing Sage in before closing it again.

"I know this has to have been a big shock..."

"You think? I have to tell you, that apparition needs to take lessons on manifesting itself from Holmes, because believe me, when he was fucking me earlier, his cock was as solid as a rock. Oh God, why am I lashing out at you? You weren't the one who lied to me."

"Technically, I was a part of the lie. And lash out all you want. You've been under a terrible strain, and then you get confronted with the fact that the man you've fallen in love with didn't enter this world in the usual way."

Seeing Sage's earnestness, Rachel began to breathe a little more calmly. But still… "How can I trust him?" she wondered aloud.

"I've known Holmes longer than he's known himself. That man out there has evolved far more than I could ever have imagined. When he says he loves you? He means it. When he says he'll give up his life to save yours? He means it. Just know that if you can't forgive him, he'll die a little inside, but he'll continue to exist. I'm starting to believe they're out to stay. I don't think they could go back, even if they wanted to. It seems a trip from inside one of my manuscripts through the veil is one-way only. So, if you really think you can't forgive him, then let him protect you and send the Ripper to hell once and for all and walk away. Please don't play with his emotions."

"How do you know any of that?" she asked, still shaken, but wanting to believe.

Sage smiled. "Because I created him—his looks, his background, everything. And he's become so much more. They all have. He and Roark look exactly the way I wrote them—so you can thank me for that big dick." Rachel smiled in spite of herself. "Oddly, Felix doesn't look anything like my description. I sort of described him as looking like Agatha Christie's Poirot."

Rachel laughed. "Boy, did you get that wrong."

"I know. And I know it's hard to understand and hard to forgive the lie, but for what it's worth, I do believe him when he says the reason he didn't tell you was because he was afraid you'd leave. And admitting that anything frightens him is difficult for a Dom like him. He expects himself to be your rock, your protector, your shelter in any storm. And now he's had to admit, he isn't perfect, he screwed up and he's dying inside waiting for you to forgive him."

"Or maybe he was just afraid I'd tell someone; maybe he doesn't give a damn about me and I'm just good for a fling."

"Is that what you're afraid of? I can tell you categorically that isn't it. None of us has ever been afraid of that. Holmes hasn't had sex outside of Baker Street since his arrival. He's very careful as I think he's afraid he doesn't have much to offer. Even if you did betray our secret, who would believe you? All of the books, audiobooks, reviews, everything—it all reflects the current characters. But I promise it never even crossed anyone's mind that we couldn't trust you."

Rachel sat down on the bed next to Sage, sighing

and emotionally spent. "I suppose it explains why none of you ever questioned my sanity."

"When that thing came through the door after you, it was clear that something supernatural was happening. And we will get to the bottom of it. We won't let it have you. I believe Holmes would go back through the veil, dragging that thing with him to make sure you were safe."

Rachel was surprised at the way her heart seized in her chest at the idea of a life without him.

"You love him, don't you?"

"I don't know," Rachel lied.

"Don't you?" asked Sage. "If I were you, I'd use this to your advantage…"

"What do you mean?"

"I wouldn't ask him to grovel, because honestly it cost him to admit he fucked up, but I'd get some custom corsets and maybe a little grace around swearing and the like."

Rachel laughed. She really did like the erotic romance author.

"From that place called the Dark Garden?"

"That place is amazing, and Louis really is the best if you can just get past his condescending attitude towards submissives."

Rachel laughed again. It occurred to her that she hadn't laughed like this in a long time. "Can I ask you something?"

"Anything at all. Selfishly, I want this thing to work out between the two of you. One, because I'm a romance writer and I love a happily ever after. Two, because Holmes really does love you. And three, because it would be nice to have someone I can talk to who's in the same position as me."

"Since you don't know how they got out, do you worry that one day you'll wake up alone?"

Sage nodded. "I did at first. But Roark told me no power in this world or any other would take him away from me. And I decided if something did happen, I didn't want to have wasted any of the time I had with him."

As Rachel pondered those words, Sage stood up to leave. Her hand on the door, she paused. "The guys have ordered food, as Holmes wants to share with Roark what you learned from your friend. It might be helpful if you were there. If you don't want to come out, I'll bring you something to eat. If you can't forgive Holmes, I'll understand. But we will figure this out and we will still protect you."

Rachel watched her leave, the door closing silently behind her. Sage was right, she decided. Regardless of her feelings for Holmes, she needed to be a part of the discussion and whatever plan they might be putting together. And if she was honest with herself, she wanted to be close to Holmes.

She washed her face and ran a brush through her

hair, pulling it back into a high ponytail, then went to join the people who had promised to protect her. She was keenly aware that if anyone could, it was these men.

When she entered the room, Holmes stood up, looking nervous. She bet that wasn't an emotion he was overly familiar with. "Where would you be most comfortable sitting?" he asked.

Seeing his anguish, her heart almost broke in two. His pain at the thought of having lost her was palpable. She wouldn't make him grovel, but she would make him regret lying to her—no, that wasn't really what he'd done. He hadn't told her everything, but could she say if the situation was reversed, she'd have done anything differently? She couldn't honestly say she would have. Maybe it was better to take Sage's advice—get some concessions and maybe a beautiful corset or two. That was the ticket, much more practical.

"Stay where you were. It's not like you have cooties," she said, sinking down into the sofa next to him. She would have sworn she could feel the relief rolling off of him. She wasn't ready to cuddle up with him, but she had to admit—if just to herself—that she wasn't going anywhere.

"Holmes was telling us that you now believe this thing is Jack the Ripper trying to get back into the world," said Roark, bringing her back to the reality and the focus of the situation.

"Yes. Saoirse said there was a very real possibility that Mary Kelly was a witch, and somehow she cursed him into the mirror."

"How could she do that?" asked Sage. "From the little research I got to do, I learned that the Ripper killed his victims before he mutilated them, which I suppose was a blessing."

"Saoirse thinks she held herself between the two worlds and then cursed him, casting him into the mirror," said Rachel, avoiding looking at Holmes.

As much as she wanted to, she didn't know if she could forgive him. He'd made her feel like a fool. Oh, but who was she kidding? Of course, she was going to forgive him. How could she not? She loved him and knew there would never be anyone else. And like Sage, she didn't want to waste too much time being angry in case whatever had thrust him into this world decided to take him back. But there was her pride to be considered. After all, he had scolded her several times about not telling him the entire truth when he was doing the same, but on a far grander scale.

"She also told us," said Holmes, drawing her back out of her reverie, "that the feeling people had of being watched was because the Ripper had been looking out, learning, and biding his time. When the mirror cracked, he escaped, latching onto the first person he encountered, which was Rachel."

"Saoirse thinks it's growing in strength, since it is gaining shape and solidity and it spoke last night."

"Does it want to possess you?" asked Sage, innocently, provoking a low growl from Holmes.

Roark rolled his eyes. "For God's sake, Holmes, she meant as in taking over her body, not possessing her like you want to do."

"We didn't get that far. I was thinking we need to call her again or go up to see her in Limerick," said Rachel.

"Mary Kelly was from Limerick," supplied Sage. "Maybe she has descendants who could help."

Rachel shook her head. "No, her family left Ireland and moved to Wales. That's where her life took its first tragic turn. She lost her husband in a mining accident and had to fend for herself, eventually turning to prostitution, which led to her fatal encounter with the Ripper."

"We can go up to Ireland if you want," offered Holmes.

"That might not be a bad idea," Rachel mused. "Perhaps Roark and Sage could accompany me, or maybe Watson?"

Honestly, she didn't want anyone else to go with her but him, but she refused to just roll over, spread her legs and let him off without a hitch. How dare he not tell her the truth? How dare he not trust what they had if he believed it was real? But he did seem to understand he'd fucked up, and not just by keeping secrets. According to Sage, it wasn't that he didn't trust her, it was that he hadn't had faith in her… in them.

"Roark and Sage need to stay here, as does Watson…"

"There's no reason Roark and I can't go with her if that's what Rachel wants, and Watson could probably get the time as well."

"That's enough, Sage," said Roark with a benign, but stern, look on his face. "The next time you try to stick your nose into what's between them, you'll find yourself facing a corner with a well-spanked bottom."

Sage quieted down, but Rachel watched as her new friend blushed a pretty shade of pink. She couldn't help but remember the feelings of arousal that often coursed through her system when Holmes spoke in a similar way to her. It was obvious Roark adored Sage; it was also just as obvious who the dominant partner was in their relationship. Rachel wanted what they had and was beginning to understand what Holmes had meant by an intimacy that went beyond the bedroom walls.

"It's getting late. I think it's best we get some sleep before this thing shows up." Roark stood, offering his hand to his wife. Rachel was beginning to notice how solicitous he was of Sage—always helping her up, getting her chair, taking care of her.

"I don't know that two of us will be better able to handle it than one," said Holmes. "There's no need for you to come back."

"No need other than not leaving a friend to face whatever or whoever that thing is by himself," said Roark.

"You two do realize I'm sitting right here, and I've been coping with it far longer than either of you," said Rachel. The words escaped her before she could halt them.

"Enough, Rachel," Holmes warned. "You can lash out at me if you need to. You will not get snarky with Roark."

"Want to bet?" she challenged. She just couldn't stop pushing him.

"Do you need me to add some more sting to your tail?" Holmes growled.

"You're not my Dom," she countered.

"That's right," said Sage. She yelped as Roark's hand connected with her ass. "Well, he kind of blew that out of the water when he didn't tell her before they became intimate. She doesn't even have a collar."

"She has a point, Holmes. If I were you, I'd remedy that as soon as possible and before you go to Ireland. And I'd get a ring put around her finger as well. Boodles, downstairs, is very accommodating. Come along, Sage, before you get yourself into more trouble." Roark took his wife by the elbow. "We'll be back before two."

Holmes handed him one of the key cards. "You

should probably have this. Obviously, Gabe can get in here without assistance, and Rachel won't be leaving the room without me." When they'd left, he turned to her. "Thank you for allowing us to continue to help you. Whatever happens between us is your decision, and I will abide by your wishes. Why don't you try to get some sleep? I'll be in here making arrangements for tomorrow, and I'll join you before that thing shows up. I'd appreciate it if you'd leave the door open so I can hear you, but if you'd prefer to close it, I'll understand."

As Rachel turned to leave, he added, "Rachel, if you think there's even a chance that you'll give us another shot, we can slow it way down. And if I've turned you off D/s, we can even have a vanilla relationship if that's what you want."

She didn't say a word, just continued into the room, closing the door behind her. She needed some distance from him. Alone for the moment, she pulled off her clothing, folding it neatly and putting it away. Naked, she stood in the middle of the room, trying to decide what to do. What was wrong with her? Why couldn't she just find the grace to tell him she would forgive him? That wanted to have what Roark and Sage had—for however long she could have it?

She knew she should crawl into bed and try to sleep. She thought about putting on the sheer nightgown Sage had loaned her, and also considered just getting into bed naked. But as she stood there debating what she should do on so many levels, the decision came to her with a clarity she had rarely known before.

CHAPTER 15

He'd hoped against all common sense that she could forgive him—that she could live with what he was. Maybe that's why he'd restricted his prior sexual encounters to those covered by a D/s contract. When the door had closed, he'd felt like she was closing the door on any chance of any kind of reconciliation.

He sat down at the desk, opened his laptop and began to go through emails, doing some preliminary research on ways to get rid of this thing. Because whatever else he did in his life, he meant to ensure that Rachel was left in peace.

The sound of the bedroom door opening caught his attention, and he swiveled around in the desk chair. If he lived to be a thousand, he would never forget the sight of Rachel as she lounged in the doorway, leaning against it. She wasn't naked; she wasn't wearing Sage's nightgown or whatever she normally slept in. Instead, she was wearing his shirt.

God, she was stunning.

"I'm not sure you understood the basics of the 'we're taking a step back and not rushing into anything' idea," he murmured.

"That's not true. Don't get me wrong, I'm still pissed at you, but I forgive you. I can't honestly say that I wouldn't have done what you did, but it still doesn't make it right and I don't have to like it. But Sage said something to me when I asked her if she didn't worry about something dragging Roark back into the book."

"Is she worried about that? Are you?"

"Holmes, could you please shut up and let me have my moment?"

"Watch that bratty mouth, Rachel." He felt his smile grow fierce. His blood, which had gone ice-cold at the thought of losing her, rushed back through his system, fired up in a way that only she could make it. "But go ahead and tell me what Sage said."

"She said that if it happened, she didn't want to have wasted even one minute being worried about it. I decided she was right. I don't want to miss even one minute of being with you."

He crossed over to her, gripping the front of her shirt, *their* shirt, in his hands and hauling her against his chest. Eagerly, his mouth came down on hers. His tongued surged past her lips and teeth, dominating as it slid along hers and tangled with it. Rachel moaned into his mouth and leaned against him. This was what he wanted. If something from another plane of existence wanted her, it would have to go through him first. And that would never happen.

Wrapping his fist in her hair, he tilted her head back, studying her face. "You forgive me?" he asked. She nodded. "You put me through hell, Rachel. And you kneed me in the nuts. Do I need to tell you the kind of hell there'll be to pay if you ever even think about doing that again?"

A small smile played at the corners of her mouth. "I didn't do any permanent damage, did I? Because I'd never forgive myself if I did." She rubbed against him like an alley cat in heat.

"I think I can come up with a way for you to do a thorough inspection and atone at the same time. Take off the shirt, Rachel." She complied. When she was naked, he said, "Now get me naked."

Her tiny grin lifted into a generous smile that lit up the entire room. Slowly, teasingly, she brought her hands down from his neck and began to meticulously unbutton his shirt. As each button revealed the skin of his chest, she kissed, nipped and licked her way down.

When she reached his waistband, she tugged his shirt tail out of his trousers and slid the garment off his broad shoulders, smoothing her hands down his arms as she did so. She tossed it onto the couch, out of the way. He leaned over and grabbed a pillow, tossing it onto the floor. She unfastened his fly, then sank gracefully to the floor. Sliding his trousers and boxers down past his rump, she freed his cock. He stepped out of both, and those too were tossed away.

Rachel rocked back and waited. Something caught in his chest at the sight of her. She was submitting, showing him in a way she knew he would understand, that they would be okay; that he hadn't destroyed the precious thing they were building together.

His cock jutted away from his body, completely engorged. She looked up at him, and he smiled in answer to her silent question. Her tongue darted out between her lips, and she licked the drop of pre-cum that was weeping out of the slit. She began to deposit light kisses that felt like fluttering butterfly wings all up and down his cock. This was not going to help him maintain control.

As her face approached his groin, she nuzzled the base of his shaft and turned her attention to his balls. They were heavy and hard, threatening to empty themselves. It was all he could not to fall on her, tipping her onto her back so he could shove his cock inside her.

"Lean back and put your hands on the floor behind you. Arch your back."

Rachel smiled and did as he commanded, thrusting her tits out as an offering. With her legs spread wide, he had a clear, unobstructed view of her glistening pussy. She was wet and he had yet to touch her. He'd have to invest in some truly beautiful nipple clamps for her. Her pebbled peaks were the perfect size and shape to be clamped. He could have her sit naked at his feet at Baker Street or in his lap up in the lounge. Maybe since she was new to the lifestyle, he'd show her around and show her off wearing only the jewelry with which he'd adorned her body.

Holmes walked around her and marveled that she was his; that she knew the truth and that she wanted him in spite of everything. He vowed to himself that he would never deceive her again. Standing behind her, he leaned down, capturing her mouth with his as he cupped her beautiful breasts. They'd only been together the one time earlier in the day, yet he felt as if they'd always been together. Already he knew her body so well, and there was a sense of satisfaction and ease that came with being with her.

He kissed his way down her chin and her throat. Already, her nipples had hardened, begging for his mouth's attention, and he meant to give them what they desired. He took one turgid tip between his thumb and forefinger, rolling it with just enough tightness to give it some edge as his mouth closed over the other. He suckled strongly and deeply, watching as her back arched even more. Unconsciously, she began to move her hips. He gave her nipple the edge of his teeth as he let it pop out of his mouth before moving to the other one.

Holmes lifted her in his arms and carried her to the bed, where he laid her out and stretched out beside her. Enjoying the delicious sight of her, he ran his finger from the hollow of her throat down the midline of her body, teasing her belly button. He did the same with her clit, teasing and traveling down to her wet, ripe pussy. He inhaled her arousal. God, she smelled sweet.

Rachel shivered in need as she reached for him.

"No, Rachel, hands above your head. I want you to hold onto the headboard. You don't let go until I tell you that you can. Do you understand?"

"Yes, Sir."

He traced her labia, coming close to but not quite touching the entrance to her core. Rachel moaned but she didn't move her hands. He trailed his fingers past her pussy to her tightly puckered back entrance. She clenched her bottom, and he smiled. He would bet a substantial amount of money that he would be the only man to know the ecstasy of taking Rachel's ass. And he sure as hell meant to do so.

"You're mine, Rachel." She nodded. "Say it."

"Yours," she said on an inhaled breath as he brought his hand back up to play in the wet folds of her sex.

His fingers teased around her pussy and clit, never actually touching them, making her breath become shallow and thready. His poor little sub had no idea of all the dirty, nasty things he planned to do to her. He'd make her crave each and every one.

As he brushed his thumb across her swollen nub, Rachel shuddered, her cream coating his hand. Ah. She was trying to hold back from him.

"No, Rachel. Your orgasms belong to me. Unless I tell you otherwise, you are to indulge in all the pleasure I give you and reward me with the sound of your climax."

He brought his hand back up to her clit, rolled it between his finger before pinching it and giving it a hard tug. As he did so, her entire body shook as the first orgasm overtook her, stunning in its speed and power.

His hand moved down to her pussy, and he shoved two fingers up into her wet heat, thrusting in and out before pressing down hard on her clit—sending her careening over the edge a second time. He'd never known a woman as responsive to his touch as Rachel. He stroked her gently as she came back down, withdrawing his fingers when she'd settled and bringing them to his mouth. He sucked them clean, enjoying the taste.

Locking eyes with her, he rolled between her legs, inching his body down so that his face was at her mound. Grinning like the Cheshire Cat, he nuzzled her clit before burying his face in her pussy. He tongued her throbbing clit and licked down to her pussy. He nibbled her swollen labia, using his tongue to lap up the honeyed cream that wept from her cunt. Her body was shivering, preparing to come again for him. He tongue-fucked her, his massive arms wrapped around her thighs, ensuring she couldn't get away from him. Rachel came a third time as Holmes made a meal of her until her body quieted again.

"All fours, Rachel," he said, rocking back on his knees. "Present that pretty ass to me."

"Holmes?" she squeaked.

He knew what troubled her. "Not tonight, but soon. You're mine—every single part of you. I will have your ass, and I will make you love it."

"Maybe I should have made that a hard limit."

Holmes swatted her butt cheeks, which still showed a little bit of color from earlier in the day.

"Too late. Besides, Roark is right. Tomorrow before we leave for Ireland, we'll go down to Boodles and pick out a ring and a collar for you."

She glanced over her shoulder at him. "You can't ask me to marry you."

"Did you hear a question in what I said, sub?" He loved the way her body responded to specific tones and words. Calling her his 'sub' in a deep, dark voice earned a delightful, visceral reaction. "You'll wear my ring and my collar, or there will be discipline. Do I need to bring an extra pillow for you to sit on?" he growled.

"No, Sir."

"Ring and collar, sub."

"Yes, Sir," she said, tears glistening in her eyes.

Holmes came up behind her, letting his cock rest in the cleft of her ass as he ran his hands down her spine. He widened his strike to caress her shoulders before sliding down her sides, lingering at her nipped-in waist. He stroked down to her ass and caressed it, leaning forward to kiss the small of her back.

Then he reared up behind her. Gripping her hips, he held her close, steadying her as he lined up his cock. Holmes slowly pressed forward, the swollen head of his cock parting her labia and beginning to breach her. He could feel her shake as he worked his dick inside her. He pushed in, pulled out and pushed in again—short, shallow thrusts to tease, torment and prepare her. Again and again, he teased her, withdrawing until only the tip was inside her before fucking back in again.

He retreated a last time, then he surged forward, driving his cock all the way to the end of her sheath until he was buried balls deep in her, groaning as he did so.

"I'm so glad I didn't damage that thing," she quipped and then yelped as his hand landed a harsh slap to her backside.

"Careful, brat. I just might decide you're more in need of getting spanked than getting fucked."

"Are the two mutually exclusive? As I recall this afternoon, they weren't."

Clearly she wasn't afraid of him.

CHAPTER 16

Pleasure and pressure filled her, tempered with the bit of pain from the swat to her backside. She meant what she'd said. If she'd permanently damaged his cock, she'd never forgive herself. He stayed tight up against her ass, not moving except for the throbbing dick he had buried in her. He reached under her and played with her clit—thumb and fingers, working in concert to bring her to orgasm again.

"Please, Holmes, I want to come with you."

He chuckled evilly. "Not to worry. I'll see to that."

Holding her hips forcefully, he dragged his cock back before slamming it back into her. He pounded into her, plunging deep and then withdrawing. Fucking her hard, so that she understood what it meant to be possessed by him. His hips rocked back and forth in a strong, powerful rhythm, driving deep each time he surged forward.

Holmes thrust into her again and again, deep and hard, as his cock hit the sweet spot in her pussy. One of his hands ran up her spine, pressing on the nape of her neck and encouraging her to lower her torso onto the mattress so that her ass was the highest point of her body.

Pleasure rocketed through her system as she called his name. He wrapped his arm around her waist, holding her tight as he slammed into her over and over, harder and faster until he sent her over the abyss again. All the while, he held himself tight against her, flooding her sheath with his cum—its soothing warmth bathing her ravaged pussy.

He eased out of her, withdrawing gently, as if he knew her body would feel his loss. He rolled to his back, pulling her close. She snuggled against him, totally sated. How could she have ever thought she'd give this up?

"For the record?" he said. She looked up at him. "I love you, and I said it first."

She smiled, happier than she'd ever been. It seemed insane to feel so good, especially since there was some specter of Jack the Ripper that had attached itself to her for some unknown reason. Yet she couldn't deny what was blossoming between her and Holmes.

"I love you too, but I won't hold you to…"

Her offer of a way out was cut off as his hand connected with the sensitized flesh of her backside.

"Finish that thought, much less that sentence, and I will spank your ass silly."

"Yes, Sir," she purred. "Does Boodles have earrings?"

Holmes looked down at her, confused. *Good*! She wanted to keep him off-kilter and on his toes.

"Yes. If you want earrings to go with your collar…"

"No, I need to buy Sage an appropriate thank-you gift," she said.

"For what?"

"For creating you with such a monstrous dick and the ability to know how to use it."

Holmes began to laugh before rolling off the bed, leaning back over and scooping her up again. She wrapped her arms around his neck and wondered when she'd become so comfortable with being carried. He brought her into the shower.

Until now, the idea of bathing with someone had never really appealed to her. But Holmes made the thought luxuriously enticing. He adjusted the shower to the perfect temperature and pulse, then began to soap her body with a soft, natural sea sponge. Gently, he washed her clean, shampooing and conditioning her hair as she moaned and sighed under his ministrations.

Turning off the water, he helped her out and

grabbed a soft, fluffy towel. He took his time drying her, running the soft cloth all over her skin, warming and soothing it at the same time.

"I thought the sub was the one who served the Dom."

He chuckled. "That's a popular misconception. We Doms call it aftercare, but it's the same thing. Like I said before, D/s is an exchange, but it's an equal exchange in many ways. Each partner worships and cares for the other. The power is a misnomer. Dominance and submission are more like yin and yang—each of us giving to the other what they need."

"And what is it you think I need from you?" she asked softly.

"My strength, my protection and my passion."

"Fair enough. What do you get from me?"

"Your trust, your gentleness and your beauty."

"What about love?"

He smiled. "That's the thing we share. It belongs to both of us in equal measure." He kissed her gently, letting his emotions roll over her and wrap her in his need for her. "Come on, love, let's get dressed. Last night is the last time that thing gets to look at my woman. Roark and I mean to confront it in the other room. If it's coming, let it, but I'll be damned if it robs you from being able to relax and sleep in our bed."

"What do you expect Sage and me to do while you and Roark take this thing on?"

"Exactly as you're told. We don't want you alone and vulnerable, so you'll be in the room with us. Watson is coming up, and he'll be behind the two of us and in front of the two of you."

"You do know you're just this side of a Neanderthal, don't you?"

He chuckled. "Sweetheart, I crossed that line a long time ago and am firmly entrenched on the other side."

∼

After they were dressed, they went into the sitting room and curled up on the couch together, each of them with a laptop. She was trying to find out as much as she could about obsidian, mirrors, the Ripper and Mary Kelly while Holmes worked on setting up their trip to Ireland.

"How do you want to get to Limerick? That's where your friend lives, right?"

"Actually, she lives outside the city. And what do you mean, how do I want to get there?"

"We can take a plane or drive. There's a train as well, but it's a lot longer and I'm not fond of the idea of being on the move when that thing shows up."

"The idea of flying doesn't really appeal to me; I'm not sure why. Normally I like to fly, but sort of like you with the train, I just don't think I want to be up in the air if it decides to come calling."

"The car it is. I have my Range Rover downstairs. Depending on what happens tonight…"

"Do you think it will be more aggressive?"

"I think it's getting stronger, and I take issue with it calling you a whore. But we may be keyed up afterwards. Taking a drive through the English and Irish countryside might be nice, but it's a long drive."

"That actually sounds good. Any chance that Range Rover of yours has the panoramic sunroof?"

"But of course."

"Sunroof to see the stars above, fresh air and country roads with the man I love… Let the Ripper come. I'll kick his ass so we can get started."

"You will stay behind Watson, but yes, it does sound like a rather nice first date. I think we should see if we can get the Savoy to pack us some food to take with us."

"Perfect—a little demon ass-kicking, good food and an evening under a starry sky."

Holmes chuckled and went about getting things arranged so they'd be ready to go.

"I think Mary Kelly is the key to this thing," she said as she joined him, leaning against the solid, muscular mass that was his body.

"How so?"

"Think about it. This thing, if it's the Ripper like we believe, didn't show up until after I had the eerie incident at Mary Kelly's room—which is the last known place the Ripper was believed to have been.

No one ever saw or heard from him again. The killings stopped. The mirror you saw had a crack in it. I know that crack wasn't there when I was in that room. There are rumors that Mary was a witch or at least dabbled in the magickal arts. What you said about Sherlock Holmes… After you eliminate everything else, even the improbable is most likely the answer. I know it's hard to believe something as fantastical as a witch casting an evil person's spirit into a mirror…"

"You're saying that to the man who, until a little more than a year ago, only existed in the pages of a book?"

Rachel had moved around to where she was standing in the circle of his arms, her back to his front, spooning like they did when they slept, or napped, or just talked in bed, She looked back and over her shoulder at him. "Point taken."

"But Holmes was right, and so are you. It may not be something we could take to the Crown Prosecutor, but that doesn't mean it isn't what happened. And here's where you have to deal with the cop. What happened to his body? They found Mary Kelly alone in a locked room."

"But don't you see? That fits too. The room was locked from the inside, meaning he never left. One of the things I want to ask Saoirse is, if Mary cast the Ripper into the mirror, would his body have gone with him? And if so, where is it now?"

"I was just messaging with Gabe and mentioned our trip. He said he'd have them give us a basket to take with us. He'll bring it when he comes up."

Rachel sat up and turned to look at him. "If only you, Roark and Felix came out of Sage's books, does Gabe know about you?"

"No. And it's a growing concern for all of us. Gabe has proven to be a good friend and we are, in essence, lying to him by keeping him in the dark. We've talked about it numerous times, and all agree he deserves to be told…"

"I don't think he'd betray your secret either, but as far as I can tell, none of you are sleeping with him, which decreases the sense of urgency about doing so. I think all of us—and I do think Sage and I have a stake in this—need to be on board."

"I agree. I can't speak for the others, but for me, it isn't about worrying he'll 'out' us, so to speak. It's more that I've come to rely on him as a friend. And if he chose to reject me and end the friendship, I would miss his company."

"We'll make it work. Maybe knowing Sage and I know and are okay with it will help him."

Holmes' chuckled. "They will have a field day at Baker Street if the three of us go in together. Without exception, if we come in at the same time, someone calls out that Holmes and Watson are on the floor and the game is afoot."

Rachel laughed. "Well, you do have to admit, it's

kind of funny. But what will they do when your evil nemesis is revealed?"

"When Dr. Moriarty is adorned only in nipple clamps with a chain hanging between her beautiful breasts and another chain leading down to a clamp around that pretty little pearl between her legs, they'll be so green with envy, they won't know what to do with themselves."

Rachel was a bit taken aback. "You'd want me naked in front of other men?"

"It's different in a lifestyle setting. It's not like anyone would touch you. But yes, I'd like to be able to show you off. I want people to know I have the most beautiful, fuckable sub in the place."

Rachel blushed, but found she wasn't as opposed to the idea as she thought she should be.

"But we can work our way up to that. And if it's a hard limit?" He shrugged his shoulders. "As long as you understand and accept that that's the way I feel, I can be content with that."

She leaned over and kissed him. "I'm not saying it's a hard limit."

Holmes grinned. "Good to know. I will protect you, Rachel. Always."

"Even from myself?" she teased.

"Especially from yourself."

There was a knock on the door, before they heard a key card being inserted. Roark and Sage entered the room. The smile on Sage's face was almost beatific.

"I'm so glad to see you both," she said.

"What she means is, she's so glad to see you both sitting together. I told you Holmes wouldn't let her go. You didn't write the man as a fool, and he hasn't proven to be one since we've been out. I always thought you might give him his own spin-off series."

"I thought about it a couple of times, but they just wanted me to churn out Roark Samuels novels and they paid well, so I did. So, what's the plan?" asked Sage.

"The plan, quite simply," said Rachel, "is for the two testosterone-laden cavemen here to put us up against a wall with Gabe standing between us and them as a kind of last stand. I'm not sure, but I think they'll be issuing guns to each of us with a single bullet so we can do ourselves in, in order to save ourselves from the Ripper's evil defilement."

Sage laughed, while Holmes and Roark growled in unison.

"Not funny, Rachel," said Holmes.

"What part of the plan did I fail to cover? Okay, the single bullet thing was added for dramatic effect, but what exactly do the two of you plan to do?"

Before they could answer, there was another knock, and Watson cracked open the door. "Everybody decent?" he called lightheartedly.

"Knock it off, Gabe," snarled Roark.

Watson joined the group, carrying a sizable, old-fashioned picnic basket. With him came a well-dressed man of average height and build, but in an impeccably tailored suit. He was about the same age as Watson, but not as heavily muscled. In his hands he was carrying a large, flat box.

"Rachel, I'd like to introduce you to Charles. He works downstairs in Boodles. They have the most exquisite things. He happened to be doing some inventory. After I spoke with Holmes earlier, he found something appropriate for you." He hefted his picnic basket. "By the way, this is the food the kitchen packed for you. They're baking bread now so if you swing by whenever you're ready to leave, they'll have it ready for you."

Charles stepped forward. "Mrs. Samuels, so good to see you this evening." He turned to Rachel, "And I assume you are Rachel Moriarty. Gabriel tells me you've agreed to take our DSI Holmes on. You two do know you'll have to come in costume to the Halloween party, don't you? In any case, Gabriel asked if I could bring up some rings and collars. We guesstimated on the ring-size, but our Watson is quite adept at noticing details."

He withdrew a smaller box from inside the larger one, revealing a number of fabulous rings on display. Rachel gasped.

"We can, of course, design something for you, but Watson seemed to think there was a bit of urgency and suggested you might like something from our vintage selection. These are not pre-owned rings, but rather ones that were either created long ago or are based on designs originating from the late eighteen-hundreds."

"These are incredible!" She turned to Holmes. "But I don't need anything this fancy."

"Think of it as nipple clamps you can wear in public."

Rachel blushed and laughed. "I take it Charles knows Baker Street?"

"I do indeed, ma'am, and it is my pleasure to help our fellow members with jewelry of all kinds."

Rachel reached for a stunning creation, one with a large oval white diamond in a platinum, halo setting, surrounded by a band of smaller round sapphires and emeralds. "This is gorgeous."

Before she could pick it up, Holmes interceded. Holding her left hand in his, he placed the beautiful ring on her finger. It was the perfect fit.

Charles smiled. "An excellent choice. This ring is from the Art Deco era and is one-of-a-kind. The setting is platinum and features an almost flawless 2.5 carat center stone in an oval cut, set in a halo comprised of round stones of a similar quality. The side stones on the shank are a marquise cut. The matching band also has diamond stones in both round and marquise cuts in a leaf and milgrain design."

Rachel just stared at it, completely speechless. She started to remove it. "It's too much."

"I will decide if it's too much," Holmes assured

her as he stopped her from taking it off.

"Which is Dom-speak for, you will never know how much it costs," quipped Sage.

Watson shook his head. "I only hope if I ever find the right woman, she'll be as practical as you two. With my luck, she'll want the crown jewels."

"That settles which ring," said Holmes. "My credit card is on file with the hotel."

"As a close friend to both Mr. Samuels and Watson, the Savoy will of course extend you every courtesy. We can just add it to your bill, to be settled when you leave." Holmes nodded. "Then as we have your ring, let's look at collars. I have to say there are going to be a lot of subs at Baker Street who will envy you. A good many of them tried to set their caps for DSI Holmes, but he was an elusive catch."

Rachel smiled as Charles showed the selection of exquisite submissive collars to Holmes. His hand moved immediately to the one that had caught her eye.

"Gorgeous, isn't it? A double row of peacock pearls, ending in a fine blue diamond pendant. The necklace closes and locks at the back with an antique platinum lock that uses a skeleton key. It's a bit more discreet than some of our collars, but those in the lifestyle will recognize it for what it is.'"

"And what is that, exactly?" asked Rachel.

"Why, DSI Holmes' sign of ownership," replied Charles.

CHAPTER 17

After Charles left, Rachel eyed Holmes speculatively. He hadn't really expected her to let that comment go without a fuss, but she said nothing, merely turned and lifted her hair so he could place the collar around her neck.

"We'll have a collaring ceremony if you like, either at the wedding or separately," he said, kissing the nape of her neck.

"You're wearing a wedding band, Holmes," she said, calmly.

"Absolutely—nothing would make me prouder or give me more pleasure."

"If you two are through canoodling, do we have a plan for tonight?" asked Watson. "Are we any closer to knowing what that thing is?"

Holmes gestured for Watson to join them as he sat in one of the large wingback chairs, drawing Rachel into his lap. The fact that she had accepted the collar and curled against him without any fuss pleased him more than he cared to admit. If this thing thought it was going to hurt or take Rachel away from him, he meant to disabuse it of that notion.

"Roark and I went to Mary Kelly's room earlier today."

"That's the last victim of Jack the Ripper, right?"

Holmes nodded. He caught Watson up on all they'd learned and deduced so far, including their theory that the disembodied spirit of the Ripper had attached itself to Rachel, growing stronger the longer it remained outside the mirror that had once trapped it. They explained what Saoirse had told them about witches and Mary Kelly too.

"It's entirely possible she banished the Ripper into the mirror. After all these years, he found a way out," Rachel explained.

"I don't understand one thing, though. If it followed you here," said Watson, "do you think you can truly outrun it? And won't it haunt the Savoy? Will it endanger the guests?"

Holmes shook his head. "We would never dump a malevolent spirit here on the hotel. We believe it isn't attached to a place, but rather to Rachel herself."

"That makes sense," added Sage, "because otherwise why would it have left Whitechapel?"

"I agree. I think you're some kind of tether for it. When it manifests itself, it has to be near Rachel.

That may change as it grows stronger, but my hope is we can destroy it long before that happens," said Holmes.

"How do you want us positioned?" asked Watson.

"I want Sage and Rachel with their backs to the door. You stand in front of them, and Roark and I will be in front of you."

"What's to keep it coming through the hallway door?" asked Rachel.

"So far, it's always come from outside in, which is what it did at Mary Kelly's. And I don't know how it would handle an electronic lock, but if you and Sage would feel safer sandwiched between us and Watson, we can rearrange things."

"Oooh, a sandwich between hunky men…" said Sage.

"Sage," growled Roark.

"Killjoy," she teased, making her husband chuckle.

As the witching hour approached, they took their positions. They kept the lights on, hoping it would deter or at least confound the apparition.

"Holmes? No offense to Watson, but I'd feel better behind you. Last night, that thing stopped in its tracks when it saw you," said Rachel softly.

"I'm with Rachel," said Sage.

"It might be better if I was closest to the door," agreed Watson. "If it tries to come in this way, I'll be here. And if it gets snarly, I can get the girls out."

Holmes looked his friend in the eye and tossed him his keys. "I have no idea if it'll work or how fast this thing is, but if this starts to go badly, get them out of here. Get them to my SUV, hit the lights and siren, and drive as fast and as far from here as you can and in the opposite direction of Whitechapel."

"Do you think that will that keep them safe?" asked Roark.

"I have no idea, but it's the best I can think of."

The antique clock, sitting next to the television, tick-tocked as if it hadn't a care in the world, but the five people crowded into the entryway listened intently as it counted down the minutes to the witching hour. Having changed their positions, Rachel reached up and took Holmes' hand. Sage's hand rested on Roark's belt.

"Sage might be safer in your room," Holmes told his friend. "I'm sorry I didn't think of that earlier."

Roark flashed him a grin. "I did. Trust me, it didn't go well. And as she pointed out to me, if I was in here, there was nothing to stop her from joining us anyway."

"Brave girl," said Holmes.

"Not really," said Sage. "I wasn't going to be left out. Trust me, I'm plenty afraid of whatever this thing is."

Holmes flashed her a grin over his shoulder. "I wasn't talking about the apparition—I meant Roark."

"Not funny, Holmes," said Sage as Roark chuckled softly.

As the witching hour approached, their banter died down. They all stared at the door that led out to the balcony, waiting. The clock continued counting down to whatever might be coming. When the electronic lock from the hallway into the suite clicked open, their focus switched abruptly from the balcony to the hallway.

Holmes and Roark pushed the women behind them, ready to repel the creature however they could. The door opened—but not to the entity. Instead, Felix walked in, wearing a frustrated expression.

"What the fuck!" snarled Holmes. Watson pulled Felix inside, shoving the door closed.

Roark and Holmes rearranged themselves so now the women were sandwiched between the two sets of men.

"What the bloody hell are you all doing?" demanded Felix. "I was coming in early to catch up on some work. Corinne and I have been short-handed. Another member of the staff assumed I'd be up here with my friends. I didn't have the heart to tell him I hadn't been invited."

"It's a long story and an oversight on my part," said Holmes. "Watson, if it goes badly, the two of you get Rachel and Sage out."

"I'm not leaving you," said Rachel quietly.

"Me either," said Sage.

"Not to worry. Watson and I will get them out to wherever it is we're supposed to go, whether they want to come or not," said Felix. He paused and added, "Might I ask what we're waiting for?"

"Quiet!" growled Holmes.

Just then, from the other room, they could hear the balcony door being unlocked. A waft of chilly air entered the suite.

"Bloody hell," whispered Felix.

"Literally," answered Rachel.

When nothing further happened, they waited. It didn't keep them long. The suite they were in had two doors to the balcony. It only took the briefest of moments before the lock on the balcony door into the sitting area rattled and then began to unlatch. Once again, chilly air filled the room, only this time, there was a faint, stale, fetid stench to it. The curtains, which had been drawn, ruffled and parted.

The air in front of the doorway seemed to soften, to blur as if an invisible creature had begun to uncloak its supernatural glamour. Though the shape lacked defined, hard edges, it grew somewhat more substantial, similar to unformed clay being sculpted, barely suggesting the shape of a human.

"Get out," snarled Holmes. "You can't have her."

"Whore…" it breathed.

"The hell I am," grumbled Rachel. "Leave me alone."

"Whore…"

"Rather limited vocabulary," said Roark in a slightly bored tone.

According to Sage's books, Holmes and Roark had been friends for a long time, tracing their friendship back to their days with MI-6. Which meant Holmes recognized Roark's affectation. The man might sound like he wasn't interested, but he was coiled and ready to strike.

"If something happens to me…" he whispered to Holmes.

"Ditto," was the clipped reply.

The thing hung in the air—a little bit deeper into the room than the previous night, but not advancing.

"Get out," repeated Holmes, taking an aggressive step forward. "We know who you are. You preyed on helpless women who had no family and few friends. You picked the wrong tether. Rachel is mine, and I will not surrender her to you."

The apparition hissed at Holmes, who held up his hand and turned his head as if he couldn't look in its direction. The hissing sound increased, as did the malodorous scent that filled his nostrils, but the thing retreated a pace. Holmes advanced again, this time followed closely by Roark.

Out of the corner of his eye, he saw Watson step forward, pushing the girls behind him as Felix stepped up beside him. Gabriel Watson might not have been in Sage's books, but he'd become a part of their little team—a true friend who was willing to stand with them before pure evil. When this was over, they would need to find a way to tell him. He deserved to know the truth.

Could the apparition sense that he, Roark and Felix were not originally of this world? Was there something about them that stopped it in its tracks? Or was it merely that the Ripper had preyed on vulnerable women and could now see Rachel no longer qualified?

With a final hiss, the blurred air swirled around, evaporating as it escaped through the balcony door, slamming and locking it as it fled. For a moment, the room was silent as everyone waited to be sure the creature didn't come back.

"I repeat," said Felix finally, "bloody hell! What was that? And why is it in my hotel?"

"Because everyone wants to stay at the Savoy," teased Watson.

"Not funny," said Felix. "Seriously, what are you people up to? By the way, Dr. Moriarty, I understand congratulations are in order. Beautiful ring. And a collar too. Holmes, old chap, you've outdone yourself."

Holmes turned to smile at Rachel. One look at her had him rushing to her side. She had lost all her color, her hand pressed against her forehead.

"Sweetheart?" he said, taking her in his arms.

"I'm okay. Or I will be, if you just hold me."

Holmes swept her off her feet and went into the

sitting room, occupying the large wingback and settling her safely in his lap.

"I just need a minute," she said. "I think that thing is getting stronger."

"Could be. You said it kept closing the distance between you and it at your flat. As I recall, your bed wasn't all that far away from the balcony door."

"It's a tiny flat, babe. My bed was much closer to the balcony door." Rachel leaned her head against his shoulder. "Was I the only one that could smell that thing?"

"No, the smell was bad enough when it was across the room. When I stepped forward, it got a whole lot worse."

"Would someone mind filling me in?" asked Felix.

"We think Jack the Ripper's last victim banished him into a mirror the night of her death. He escaped and is now tethered to Rachel. Holmes and Rachel are headed out to see an old friend of hers that might be able to help or at least give us some information."

"That's it in a nutshell," said Holmes. "I think Rachel and I should head out. We're both too keyed up to sleep. And I want as much time to get to Limerick and talk with Rachel's friend before this thing shows up again."

"I see you have one of our baskets to take with you," Felix noted. The man always resorted to being super-concierge when troubled. "Might I suggest you also take a couple of pillows and perhaps a blanket?"

"Thanks, Felix, that would be great," said Holmes. "My SUV is in the garage."

"Let me take the basket…"

"The kitchen told me they could pick up fresh bread," said Watson.

"Very good. I'll see to that. I'll bring your vehicle round front and load the basket, blankets and pillows inside for you. That way, you can just bring Rachel down when you're ready. Roark, do you and Sage need anything?"

"No, we're fine," Roark insisted. "That thing really is focused on Rachel. Are you sure you don't want me to accompany you, Holmes? Sage will be fine here at the hotel."

"Here they go," Holmes whispered against Rachel's ear.

"If you go, I go, Roark," said Sage, respectfully but with some vehemence.

"You will do as I tell you. I want you as far away from that thing as possible."

"Why? You said it yourself—that thing is focused on Rachel."

"For now. I'm not convinced it can follow Rachel. If not, it may decide you are far too tasty a treat to be ignored. Lord knows I do."

"And you would leave me behind defenseless?" Sage said, rolling her eyes.

"Hardly. I'm sure Gabriel and Felix would be happy to keep an eye on you."

"Before you get yourself in trouble, Sage, I think Roark should stay here just in case, as he suggested, the thing can't follow Rachel. Felix, if you could get the SUV—Watson has the keys. Rachel and I will get our things and not be far behind you."

"Very good, Holmes," said Felix, turning to Watson, who stood up.

"I'll come with you. You get the bread and other supplies, and I'll meet you out front."

The two men left, leaving Holmes, Roark, Rachel and Sage, who was curled up in her husband's lap.

"It's odd," remarked Rachel, "that it didn't feel at all strange to be sitting in your lap in front of a group of people."

"I have to tell you, it's one of the things I've always envied about Sage and Roark. Their relationship is so strong, so palpable, that it isn't just confined to their bedroom or even their rooms here at the Savoy. It's something they carry out into the world."

"Yes, but be careful when they get too comfortable and decide that if you're misbehaving they can, should and will correct you in public," said Sage.

"There's a very easy way to prevent that," remarked Roark. "Behave yourself."

Sage rolled her eyes again. "Now, where's the fun in that?"

CHAPTER 18

After Roark and Sage left, they packed their things in Holmes' duffle bag. They would only be gone overnight.

"You're taking wool trousers, a dress shirt and nice shoes? We're just driving up and back, aren't we?" Rachel asked him.

"Yes, and we'll be seeing your old college roommate and asking for her help. Don't you think it would be nice to take her out to dinner? Make sure you have your passport."

"I'm a British citizen…"

"Who was born abroad. It should be fine, but it's better to have it with us in case we need it. If it makes you feel better, I have mine with me as well."

"Ooooh, fancy," Rachel teased, amazed at how he could make all the terror she'd been feeling roll off her like water off a duck's back. "Would that be our second date? It's been so long since I dated, I think I'm doing this wrong. I get engaged and collared, then go on my first date in a car, running away from an apparition, and then take my old roommate to dinner. That's just messed up."

"Depending on who you talk to, you got spanked and fucked before you did anything else." He kissed her nose as she laughed. "But that's better than Sage."

"Oh God, do I even want to know?"

"Roark spent years barely managing to invade her dreams. When he finally got out, he only barely saved her from being murdered. She had blacked out and when she came to, she was naked in Roark's bed with a butt plug in her ass."

"You're right. All things being equal, hers was worse."

"And she got herself spanked as well, so you're in good company there."

When their things were packed, they rode down to the lobby and headed outside where Watson was waiting for them.

"Take care of each other," he said, closing the passenger side door after Rachel had climbed in.

Holmes pulled away from the Savoy and drove onto the nearly deserted streets before hitting the M-40 heading north toward Birmingham. Once they had cleared London, he reached overhead and engaged the sunroof, which opened to reveal a bright, starry night with a full moon. Holmes leaned over, turned on the heated seats and adjusted the temperature control to compensate for the chill in the air.

"Comfy?" he asked.

"Very," she said, happily. "You're very good at this whole Dom thing."

He laughed. "Because I want to be. Sage wrote me, as she did Roark, to have strong tendencies in that area of our personalities, but she hadn't counted on either of us being real and having those traits become so prominent. For me, going to Baker Street alleviated my strong libido and my need to control and serve my sub. I didn't think I'd ever find what Roark had, but Sage would tell you, I'm so much worse with you."

"I think I like that I bring that out in you. Certainly, I've never thought of myself as submissive, but then I've never been terrorized by a spirit or met a man who came out of a book."

"There's nothing wrong with being submissive, Rachel. And my guess is you'll be polite to others but only submit to me, and I am perfectly happy with that arrangement."

"And when I forget who the Dom is, you'll be happy to remind me, won't you?"

He chuckled. "I will indeed."

Eventually, Holmes persuaded her to bring a pillow forward from the back, recline the seat and sleep. She was smiling as she dozed off—warm, safe and content. Several hours later, she woke to the gentle feel of the Range Rover rocking ever so gently.

"Holmes?" she said, groggily.

"I'm right here, sweetheart," he said, lifting her hand to his lips and kissing it.

"Are we on the ferry?"

"We are. We got moved to the front of the line when they saw the Scotland Yard sticker and noticed I had my beautiful fiancé sleeping in the seat next to me." He glanced at his watch. "We shouldn't be much longer. By the time we get off, the sun should be rising, and we'll be about two hours from Limerick. We can grab some breakfast and then, depending on the time, we can meet with your friend and take it from there."

Rachel grabbed his wrist and turned it so she could look at his watch. "Saoirse was always an early riser. Once we're headed to Limerick, I'll call her. Maybe she'll meet us for breakfast."

Holmes had closed the sunroof when they'd driven onto the ferry. As he had when they were in London, he waited to open it again until they were clear of the city.

"I like this," she said, turning her face to the sun. "It's chilly, but with the seat warmer and the way you've adjusted the heat, it's nice and cozy. What's with the scowl?"

"I wish I could spare you this. If I thought it would work, I'd simply whisk you away to where that thing can't find you…"

"The problem is, I'd be worried that it would just

attach itself to someone else. I don't think your comments about Sage were all that off. I want to be back in our room at the Savoy before it comes calling again."

"I agree. I just don't like you being used for bait."

"Why don't I call Saoirse?"

"Do you know her number?" Rachel nodded. "I'll hit the phone button, and you tell the system the number to dial."

"Cool," she said, grinning.

The phone hadn't even finished its first ring when Saoirse picked up. "Who are you and what do you want?"

"That's a fine way to greet an old friend," teased Rachel.

"Rachel, are you all right?"

"Good morning to you, too," said Rachel. "I take it I didn't wake you?"

"It came again, didn't it?" she asked.

"Yes, but then it's been making nightly visits since this thing began. At least with Holmes I can sleep, and I feel a lot safer."

"He's not of this world," Saoirse said in her Irish accent, made heavier by her concern.

"He is now," Rachel reassured her. "In fact, I'm wearing his ring and his collar."

"His collar? Good lord," Saoirse laughed. "When did you get into the lifestyle?"

"Right before he spanked me for leaving the safety of the Savoy without him."

"You're in danger, Rachel. I woke up in a fright this morning. I laid out a panel for you. All the signs are there. Something from the other side has set its sights on you."

"That would be Jack the Ripper. Holmes and Roark Samuels are on my side, so I'm not liking the Ripper's chances."

"Is he listening?" Saoirse asked.

"I am. Good morning, Saoirse. We're about an hour out of Limerick and need your help. Rachel suggested we invite you to breakfast," said Holmes amicably.

"I don't think that would be a good idea. Too many people listening in. Besides, I'd like to consult my tarot with you factored in. I'm not convinced you aren't adding to the danger."

"I understand that. But as Rachel said—we're engaged and she's wearing my collar. How about if I agree to answer any questions you might have until you're feeling good about Rachel spending the rest of her life with me?"

"That's where my concern is…"

"What do you mean?" asked Rachel.

"I'm not sure being with him isn't part of the danger you're in. You come out to the farm. We can eat something here and talk without worrying about who might overhear. Do you remember the address?"

"I do. We'll be there in probably ninety minutes."

Rachel ended the call. "What's her problem with you?"

"The same as she had with Roark. As she said, we're not of this world. I mean we are now, but our origins are not what she's used to. Now that she knows that you know, she'll be a little more accepting. I think she was upset that we were together, and I hadn't told you. That doesn't make her a bad person."

"I know, but I also won't have her treating you badly because you started out life in one of Sage's books."

They drove through the Irish countryside, talking of nothing in particular. She watched him drive with a casual command of his vehicle and the road. It was easy to relax and just be with Holmes, as he was comfortable taking control and always seemed to put her needs first.

When they pulled up to the old stone farmhouse, Rachel recalled the first time she'd seen it. As long as there was no modern machinery to be seen, it was easy to imagine that you'd stepped through some kind of time portal. The house had been updated with all the modern conveniences, but the renovations had been done thoughtfully so that wires, pipes, and such were hidden away. The original structures had been built somewhere between the seventeenth and eighteenth centuries.

Hearing them approach, Saoirse walked out on

the porch to meet them. Rachel trotted from the SUV to the house and embraced her friend.

"It's so good to see you. I just wish it were under better circumstances."

"Aye. How the hell did you get involved in all of this? And what are you doing with the likes of him?" Saoirse asked suspiciously.

"Saoirse, let's get one thing straight. His name is Michael Holmes. He is a DSI with Scotland Yard. He is my fiancé, but more even than that, I love him. I don't care that he wasn't born in this timeline or plane of existence or whatever. He's here now. He loves me and if you can't be happy about that, then we won't trouble you further."

"Rachel, wait a moment," said Holmes, attempting to defuse the situation.

Saoirse smiled. "I'd forgotten what a passionate friend you are when you care about someone." She looked toward Holmes. "Do you love her? Do you deserve her?"

"Very much and probably not," he said with an easy smile.

Saoirse laughed. "Oh, I like him. Well, come along inside and tell me how this happened."

Rachel and Holmes followed her inside, and when she went to get them a cup of tea, Holmes shooed her into a seat at the kitchen table by the window and proceeded to make himself at home. Saoirse watched him for a moment, then turned to her friend.

"So?"

"I was doing a Ripper tour for a small group. We finished, of course, at Mary Kelly's. As we got ready to leave, I could see the door was open. I was sure I'd closed and locked it. But it was open, so I went back to secure it. As I put my hand on the knob, something shoved against the door, and I thought I heard a scream. I felt a gust of wind and energy come through the door and pass through my body."

Saoirse nodded. "I'll bet he wasn't expecting you to be there. That's why he's tethered to you. Didn't you tell me when you were there the mirror was fine, but when Holmes went back it was cracked?"

Holmes nodded. Once the kettle was boiling, he walked out to the SUV and brought in the big picnic basket from the Savoy. He set it on the third chair at the table.

"Apparently they thought we would starve. There should be some nice things in there to munch on."

He returned to the stove and then joined them at the table with a tray holding three mugs, the teapot and all the makings for tea. Holmes set the tray down and then opened the basket, smiling as he did so.

"This looks good. There's two loaves of bread, butter, ham and roast beef, sandwich condiments, scones—everything for not just a tasty snack but a hearty breakfast."

Once he was seated, Saoirse asked, "Did you see

or hear the mirror crack—either of you?" They both shook their heads. "Did it visit you the first night?"

Rachel nodded. "But it didn't come all the way in. and it was much more see-through. It's been gaining in substance and shape each time and coming closer and closer to me."

"What do you mean by shape?"

"At first, there was no shape whatsoever. But last night there was a kind of rectangular/humanesque shape—as if someone were molding a figure out of clay. And it's much more opaque."

"And the smell."

Saoirse turned to look at Holmes. "There was a smell?"

Holmes nodded. "A stench. It got worse the closer I got to it."

"Were you between it and Rachel?"

"I was, and it's taken to calling her a whore," said Holmes, clearly angered by the memory.

Saoirse smiled. "I rather imagine you didn't like that."

"Not one damn bit," he snarled.

"It didn't try to go through or around you?" Saoirse asked.

"No. It did move a bit to my right, but I side-stepped and then Roark was beside me."

"Interesting. It couldn't move past two from the otherworld."

"Do you think we're right? That it's some kind of Ripper apparition?" asked Rachel.

"Aye. It makes the most sense. Here's what a lot of people don't know about Mary Kelly—well, really, her mother. She was a powerful witch and healer. You have to remember, Ireland is an old country and we have long memories. The Great Hunger hadn't been gone so long; there many people remembered living through it. When the crops in this area where they lived started to fail, they looked for causes. Many believed Mary Kelly's mother had cursed them. They dragged her from her bed one night, beat her husband senseless and hanged her in their barn. When he came to and found her, he packed the children and fled to Wales, where her people had hailed from. So if Mary had the gift, she may have had enough knowledge and power to cast the Ripper into the mirror."

"I have two questions as a cop. The first is how? I mean, I know by magick, but the Ripper always killed his victims before he started in on them, and nothing in the autopsy indicates Kelly's murder was any different. Given the wounds, it couldn't have taken more than a minute for her to bleed out."

"Yes, but she could have used the last of her power to hold herself in the conduit between two worlds, where she could manipulate time in order to seek justice for herself and his other victims."

Holmes nodded. Saoirse's eyebrows rose slightly. "You're awfully accepting," she said.

"I was created by an erotic romance author and left the pages of her book as a fully realized, sentient character a little over a year ago. I'm willing to go on a little faith."

Saoirse laughed. "What's your second question?"

"What happened to the body?"

"Depending on the spell or curse, she may have tried to eliminate the possibility of him escaping the mirror by collapsing his body in on himself and sending the result into the mirror."

"So you think somehow he cracked the mirror and escaped."

Saoirse nodded. "It's the only explanation that makes sense to me."

"I lied," said Holmes. "I have a third question. How do we destroy it?"

"That, my friends," said Saoirse, "is the proverbial question, and the answer is going to take a fair amount of research. Let's go out to my dispensary. I have books out there from times long past. Maybe we can find something."

"Do you think it's still with me? That it could follow me this far?"

"Yes. Time and place don't exist for it in the same way it does for us. It's getting stronger, and I think it is feeding on your energy."

"Is that why I'm so tired? My energy just seems off," said Rachel.

"Yes, I think it comes each night, forgive me, to feed off you. I think last night Holmes and Roark stopped it. It comes closer to try and get more from you."

"And calling her a whore?" asked Holmes.

"The Ripper was a misogynist bastard who hated women. Being cast into the otherworld—not quite heaven or hell—hasn't improved his disposition. And it hasn't allowed him to move on."

CHAPTER 19

*A*s they approached the dispensary, Rachel kept her eye on Holmes. The building was made of stone, of the same era as the farmhouse. As they entered, Saoirse flipped on the light switch, illuminating the interior.

"Whoa," said Holmes. "This was not what I was expecting."

Rachel had always loved Saoirse's dispensary. You could almost feel the good that was done within these walls. She'd also loved how Saoirse was such a product of her ancestry, spiritual beliefs and training. The small building had a low, thatched roof. Inside, three of the walls had counters running along their length with open shelving above them. The shelves were filled with jars and pottery containers of various sizes and shapes—each one labeled with what was in it.

Below, the counters hung café-type curtains, concealing whatever it was Saoirse didn't want prying eyes to see. There were no overhead light fixtures. and the only windows were in the wall in which the door was placed. All along the walls were sconces that provided soft, ambient lighting. Between the door and the windows on either side were floor to ceiling bookcases, containing numerous mementos as well as books that contained, Rachel supposed, history, recipes, medicines, maybe even spells. The bookcases had locked doors with inset, antique bubble glass.

"I have a PhD in chemistry, and I make prescription compounds for people all over the UK, Canada, New Zealand and Australia. I can't be making them in a dimly lit, dirty, musty old building. I closely regulate the temperature and climate in here. It seemed the perfect place to store all of my books."

Saoirse walked to them, searching for what they needed.

"I have them organized by year. I don't think we need to look at anything after 1888. Or before 1863, which is the year we believe she was born. The books from those twenty-five years would most likely contain any knowledge she might have had. Let's gather them up and go back inside. We'll be more comfortable."

They took the books pertinent to the time period of Mary Kelly's short, tragic life and returned to the farmhouse, spending the next several hours combing over the tomes.

Throughout the day, Holmes—who confessed he felt out of his realm of expertise when it came to the supernatural and 1800s history—waited on both women. He did his share of reading, looking for anything that sounded plausible before passing it off to either Saoirse or Rachel. In between, he cooked, made sure Rachel and Saoirse had food and drink, and in general took care of them, even going out to feed the stock so Saoirse didn't need to interrupt her reading. As he walked outdoors, Rachel looked away from watching his muscular buttocks to find Saoirse grinning at her.

"That man of yours has a fine ass," said Saoirse. "And for a dominant alpha male, he's awfully solicitous of you and of me by extension."

Rachel nodded. "He is the dominant partner between us, and I've found a peace in submitting to him that I haven't known before. As he said, it's not that he doesn't value my opinion or want to know what I think; he just needs to have control. He said that's the way Sage wrote him, but I think it's because he was once a character in a book, subject to Sage's whims and the needs of her fiction. After all, he was a secondary character. I suspect having control gives him the same sense of peace that submitting to him gives me."

"Makes sense. I have to tell you, both he and Roark ruffled my feathers—not them per se, but their existence. But it's easy enough to tell that your

Holmes loves you the way Roark loves Sage—the way a woman ought to be loved and cherished. By the way, that ring and collar are stunning."

"They are, and I don't think I ever want to know what they cost."

"Will you live in your flat?" asked Saoirse.

The ability to step away from all that had been happening to her and just discuss something normal—like her fiancé, where they would live, and such details—was a welcome boon to Rachel's flagging energy.

"Doubtful. Holmes doesn't care where we live as long as we're together, but I don't want to live there—not after this. He has a row home in Chelsea overlooking the Thames. Thankfully, Sage wrote him as coming from a very wealthy family, but feeling called to serve, first in MI-6 and then with Scotland Yard."

"Is it a bit weird—being with someone who hasn't always existed in this realm?"

"Not yet, but then we've only known each other a few days."

"And yet," said Saoirse, "you agreed to marry him and accept his collar."

"You may not have noticed, but he's a bit difficult to say no to."

Saoirse laughed. "That he is, and I suspect he has a wicked hand when he thinks you need it."

Rachel felt her cheeks flush. "He does, but when

he turns his focus to pleasure, it's like nothing I've ever experienced before."

Holmes rejoined them. "Good, you two are taking a break."

"I appreciate all your help," Saoirse responded. "I'm sorry if you feel I was abrupt or impolite yesterday or earlier today."

Holmes shrugged. "No need for an apology. You care about your friend, who also happens to be the woman I love. That buys you a lot of leeway with me. Now, how do you two feel about cottage pie?"

"All right, that's it. When you get back to London, you tell your friend, Sage Matthews, to write me one just like him."

Rachel and Holmes both laughed. When he brought the bubbling casserole to the table and heaped their plates with plentiful helpings, Rachel felt as though she was getting a glimpse of her future. She leaned over to kiss him.

"Worried, sweetheart?"

"No. Just the opposite. I can see a lot of this kind of friends and family time at our home in Chelsea. I've never even seen pictures, but I just had a flash of what was meant to be."

Saoirse leaned over and squeezed her hand. "You hang onto that."

They enjoyed their dinner and Holmes cleared the table, admonishing them to go back to their research.

Less than an hour later, Rachel cried excitedly,

"Saoirse, I think I might have something about the spell Mary Kelly must have cast."

"Point of information," said Holmes. "Why do we care how Mary Kelly sent the Ripper into the mirror? Are we going to try to send it back the same way?"

"We can try, but if possible, I'd rather find a way to destroy it," Saoirse said. She looked at the book Rachel was holding. "You might be right. As she herself was already dead and had little time, this could be it. She could have asked the mirror to absorb his evil and remove him from her sight."

"How do we get rid of it?" persisted Holmes.

"I don't know. Probably the best we can do is to banish it back into something that can contain it," said Saoirse.

"Not good enough," said Rachel. "I don't want this thing to ever get out and come after somebody again." She looked at Saoirse's face and observed her body language. "You look as though you don't think this can be done."

"The problem is for a proper banishing spell, you're going to need something that belonged to the Ripper. As the spirit hasn't fully formed, it'll need something to attach to other than Rachel before you send it back. I fear that if you send it back and it is attached to Rachel, it will pull her into the otherworld as well."

"That's not happening," growled Holmes.

"There may be no other way. If it gets powerful

enough to detach itself from Rachel, it may be too strong to banish. We would need something that the Ripper was attached to—something familiar—something he left behind," said Saoirse.

"I've never been overly interested in the Ripper. There's nothing I can do for those poor women he butchered. I prefer to focus my efforts on helping the living and bringing justice to those who haven't been dead for more than a century."

"I remember reading the case files are sealed. What about the evidence?" asked Rachel.

"What about it?"

"Is there any way you could look at it or maybe borrow a piece?"

"You mean steal?" Holmes asked incredulously.

"It's not like you're going to have to go to court."

Holmes shook his head and covered her hand with his. "You're right, sweetheart. We'll get back to London and stare this thing down again. First thing in the morning, I'll leave you with Roark and Sage and go into the Yard's evidence archives and see what I can find. What am I looking for?"

"Something personal," said Saoirse. "A scarf, a hat, something he would have carried on his person."

"What about the knife he used?" suggested Rachel.

Holmes shook his head. "One of the few things I know is that no murder weapon was ever found."

"Besides," added Saoirse, "he most likely would

have had that in his hand, and it would have been banished into the mirror with him."

"So what you're saying is, this homicidal maniac that's attached itself to my fiancé has a weapon. So if it ever materializes…"

"He'll be armed," finished Saoirse.

They all seemed to notice that sun was beginning to set.

"Holmes?"

He checked his watch. "I don't think we can make London before it comes. We'll find someplace…"

"Aye, you're already here," said Saoirse. "I've a ring of fairy stones. If I cast some salt, it'll be hard-pressed to cross over. Come. I'd like to get there before dark and light a beacon fire."

Holmes looked at Rachel. "I don't have any better idea, do you?"

"No," she said. "In for a penny, in for a pound."

"Leave your watch, your mobiles, anything electronic or modern. This is an ancient place and those that abide there don't like the disruption in the elemental forces caused by modern things."

Holmes removed his watch, putting it in the basket Saoirse provided, along with his and Rachel's mobiles. Saoirse gathered what was left of the bread and added cheese, berries, cooked sausages and a surprising amount of salt to another basket. "It's a bit of a hike, and we've a long wait."

Saoirse gathered three torches, lighting them. The fragrance of sage and lavender filled the air.

"Holmes, could you grab some of that wood by the dispensary? Nothing mechanical was used to gather it, and it is all from my property."

He did so, stopping at the SUV to grab the blankets Felix had provided, before falling in behind them. Saoirse led the way, with Rachel in the middle and Holmes guarding their rear. They walked along a well-worn path, heading west and watching as the sun sank slowly behind the horizon. Surprisingly, the torches provided good light.

The sound of the sea was faint at first but became more and more distinct. As they approached a cliff, Saoirse started down a steep path that led to another level of her property. The moon cast its bright light on the ocean, making it seem inviting and menacing at the same time. Finally, they came to a ring of thirteen standing stones, set in a fairly well-defined circle. The center was surrounded by braziers, and Saoirse lit the contents.

"Here, let me have the wood," she said.

Rachel and Holmes stayed out of her way as she built a small bonfire. Its flames and sparks leapt into the air, and what had been gathering gloom became filled with light. Saoirse took the salt and spread it between the ring of stones and the ring of braziers.

"That should slow him down. Now what?" Saoirse asked.

Holmes tossed both women a blanket and then spread one on the ground.

"Now, we wait," he said. "See if you can't close your eyes and get some sleep, sweetheart," he said, pulling Rachel against his side.

She snuggled up next to him, thinking how odd it was that she felt so safe and so at home with this man that she'd joined her life with. They'd only known each other a few days, yet they fit so perfectly together. She looked over to see Saoirse smiling at her. "What?"

"If we manage to pull this thing off and send the Ripper back beyond the grave, you tell your author friend I want one of those," Saoirse said, nodding toward Holmes.

"Be careful what you wish for. All of Sage's heroes have a penchant for spanking their naughty heroines," he teased.

They sat within the protected circle, talking like old friends. Granted, she and Saoirse had been roommates, but like her, Saoirse seemed to have decided Holmes was one of the good guys. They ate the food they'd brought with them and waited as the night grew darker and darker.

The full moon became hidden behind angry clouds that started to flash with lightning contained within.

"That's interesting," said Saoirse, standing.

"What is?" asked Holmes, rising to his feet beside her.

"There's no rain predicted for several days."

"You've always said that sudden summer squalls continue to baffle modern weathermen," remarked Rachel as she joined them on her feet.

Saoirse shook her head. "No, this isn't weather. He's trying to manifest himself close to you, and he's having trouble."

A bolt of lightning struck the earth outside the circle of stones. Saoirse smiled. "With the right preparations and ingredients…"

"Ingredients?" asked Rachel.

"Aye," said Saoirse. "Things like salt, fire, white sage and the like, we might just be able to pull this off."

The night sky lit up with lightning and thunder as the apparition tried again and again to get close to them.

"It's like it's throwing a temper tantrum," said Rachel, for the first time fascinated and not afraid.

"For the record, that behavior will get you put over my knee so fast, it'll make your head spin."

Rachel laughed. "It's really pissed."

"Aye," said Saoirse. "In London, it thought it could get to you. It's probably pissed on a variety of levels. First, you get the hunky Dom here from the otherworld to protect you with his otherworld buddies providing a barrier, and now an ancient circle of stones. It has to be confused and confounded by the stones, the salt and the light. Its allies are darkness and fear and it can find very little of either within this protective circle. Yeah, it's not happy at all."

The lightning and thunder crashed all around them for close to an hour. And then as suddenly as the rainless storm had appeared, it was gone.

"Well," said Saoirse, "that was quite the show."

"It's gone," said Rachel. "Not gone, gone. But gone until tomorrow."

"Why don't we stay here and try to get a little sleep? In the morning, we'll head back to London. Saoirse, I know, it's a huge ask…"

"Are you kidding me?" she said. "You couldn't keep me away if you wanted to."

"When we get back to your house, we'll call the hotel and get you a room," said Rachel, grateful for her friend's willingness to help.

As Saoirse settled on the other side of Holmes, she said, "I know it's a long way, but I think when we confront this spirit for the final time, we do it here. I can try to trap it between the stones and the salt, and then see if we can't send it to hell once and forever."

CHAPTER 20

The trip back to London was long, but uneventful. Their time in Ireland had done Rachel a world of good. Saoirse was good for her. They laughed and talked, and Holmes enjoyed listening to them tell tales about each other. Several people on the ferry back to England remarked about the weird storm that had taken place in an isolated and consolidated place along the western Irish coast. Little did they know.

When they pulled up to the front of the Savoy, the valet came down to take their keys. Felix had managed to do the impossible and found Saoirse a room on the same floor as their own.

"Good afternoon, Ms. Madigan. I'm Felix Spenser, the Head Concierge here at the hotel. Welcome to the Savoy, and thank you for agreeing to help us. I'll take your bags up and get you settled in. Roark has ordered lunch up to their suite and thought we all might meet to go over what we know and coordinate our plan."

Felix supervised the SUV's unloading and then took charge of the luggage trolley and headed up to their floor. Holmes got Saoirse registered and then escorted the ladies up to Roark and Sage's suite.

"I don't think I'm dressed well enough to come in the back entrance to this place," said Saoirse. "I don't even think I know what a concierge does."

"In Felix's case—absolutely everything. Everybody depends on him, and he loves it."

"He's one of you, isn't he?" said Saoirse.

"Yes, he is, although according to Sage, he doesn't look anything like what she described in her original books."

"She couldn't have made him any dreamier," Saoirse said. Then she frowned. "Would you mind running a little interference for me with your friend Roark? I'm afraid I wasn't as welcoming as I might have been."

"Not to worry. I'll make sure he knows how terrific you were last night and as long as you didn't make Sage cry, he'll be fine," said Holmes, reassuringly.

"I take it he's the only one who gets to make her cry."

"And the only time it doesn't absolutely slay him is

when she's being disciplined for something, and even then it gets to him."

As they entered what was now christened the Best Seller Suite, Sage rushed to embrace Saoirse. "Rachel told me all you did for them in Ireland. We can't thank you enough."

"Why did you have to go and be so nice? Now, I really feel like a bitch."

Roark smiled and extended his hand. "No need. What you did for Holmes and Rachel wipes the slate clean. Let's get started, shall we?"

"Where's Watson?" asked Holmes.

"You guys know a Watson?" laughed Saoirse.

"We do, and he doesn't know about us—something we're going to need to remedy in the very near future," answered Roark. "We had some information from Eddy about something incongruous in the contents of Mary Kelly's room. Thank God, even back then you people were meticulous about cataloging and listing things."

"But how would Eddy get it?" asked Holmes.

Saoirse raised her hand. "Who is Eddy?"

"One of my characters who we think could leave the book if he wanted, but seems to find staying inside more comfortable," answered Sage. "He's a hacker extraordinaire. Apparently at some point, someone put the lists on microfiche. You know Eddy; if it's anywhere electronic, he can get to it."

"What did he find?" asked Rachel.

"Apparently, there was a man's pocket watch. No one seemed to think much of it at the time, but the man Mary Kelly had been living with had left her the week before."

Rachel, Holmes and Saoirse looked at each other, smiled and said at the same time: "Perfect."

The Savoy had provided a buffet for lunch, including salad, soup, sandwich makings, drinks and dessert. The drapes had been pulled, blocking the view of the Thames, and an enormous electronic whiteboard had descended from the ceiling. As they ate lunch, they went over all they'd found out with Saoirse adding what they'd discovered at her home.

"Did you hear about the unexpected and very local tempest off the western coast of Ireland?" asked Saoirse.

"Yes. The news made quite the to-do about it," said Felix.

"That was the Ripper. He couldn't get anywhere close to Rachel. We were in a ring of standing stones and then within a circle of light surrounded by salt. He was none too happy."

"I'm sure this isn't germane to anything," said Felix, "but I've always wondered, does it have to be a special kind of salt?"

Saoirse smiled. "No, any kind of salt will do, but the less refined the better, in my opinion. I have some very coarse rock salt that I use."

"Fascinating," said Felix, staring at Saoirse.

"I'll say," whispered Rachel to Holmes.

There was a knock on the door, right before it opened and Watson stepped in.

"I bid you all a good day, and ta-da!" Watson said, holding up the pocket watch.

"Jesus, Watson. Please don't tell me you stole that from the evidence locker," said Holmes.

"Of course, I did. What were you going to do—sign it out and then tell them you lost it? Or better yet, that you cast the spirit of the Ripper into it and send it back to hell?"

"Technically, as I understand it," said Felix, "if he was banished to the mirror, he wasn't in hell; he was in what many religions call the otherworld, not quite like the Christian idea of purgatory, but a place between the realms where some choose to stay. But if he was trapped, he wouldn't have been able to be free even in there."

"Give the concierge a gold star. He is absolutely right," answered Saoirse.

"So how is our trapping him in the timepiece going to be different? How do we stop him from escaping?" asked Rachel.

"I've been thinking about that all day. I don't think we trap him inside the timepiece. I think we trap him inside the standing stones, and then call him an uber to take him straight to hell." Saoirse looked around the room and laughed.

Rachel shook her head, "You're really enjoying

this whole, 'I know something you don't know,' aren't you?"

"A little bit. Actually, it's kind of nice to be around people who don't think I'm off my rocker."

"After what we saw the other night, we're really not in a position to question or mock anyone—especially someone willing to help."

"What do you people know about banshees?"

"The wailing women of Ireland who are harbingers of death?" asked Rachel.

"That's part of the legends, and the most known…"

"I was doing some research about them. There are some stories that they are also a kind of guardian angel," said Rachel.

"As well as tales of them being like Valkyries. But there's also a spell to summon them in order to capture a spirit that has escaped the Otherworld and return it—never to escape again. But to summon them for a specific soul, guess what you need?"

Rachel pointed at the pocket watch. "Something of personal importance to the soul when it was alive?"

"Precisely."

"Do you think it will work?"

Saoirse smiled. "A Madigan witch on Madigan property trying to banish an evil soul that preyed on women? I think this is right up the Banshees' alley."

"Then we're agreed. We take this thing on one more time here in London and then head to Ireland."

"I'm coming with you," said Roark.

"We're coming with you," corrected Sage.

"And this is where we exit," quipped Watson, opening the door, handing Holmes the pocket watch, and ushering Felix, Saoirse, Rachel and Holmes out into the hallway. Just before the door closed completely, there was a loud crash.

"Oh, I do hope that wasn't the Lalique vase," said Felix.

"We had a long night. Saoirse, would you mind if Rachel and I excused ourselves and tried to get some sleep? I suggest you do the same."

"I can take her to her room," offered Watson, clearly interested in the beautiful Irish witch.

"That won't be necessary," said Felix. "After all, I have her key card."

As Felix escorted Saoirse to her room, a grumbling Watson stalked back to the elevator.

"I think Saoirse just got more than she bargained for," said Rachel, smiling.

"Indeed."

Once they were back in their room, Holmes led her into the bedroom before he pushed her up against the wall. Lowering his mouth to hers, his tongue darted out, running along the seam of her lips, asking for entry. Her mouth flowered open, and their tongues tangled and danced together in the sweetest of harmonies.

"I missed you last night," she moaned against him as she felt him strip the leggings off her body.

Using the wall for leverage, he lifted her up, holding her with brute strength while he freed his cock and then slowly, unerringly and oh, so tantalizingly, lowered her onto it, letting her abundant slickness make his entry easy. Would she always respond so quickly and so viscerally to him?

"I thought I was going to die if I had to spend another moment without you impaled on my cock. Wrap your legs around me," he commanded. She willingly obeyed.

Locking his arms under her ass, he walked them to the bed and laid her carefully down on it until he was on top of her. She was trapped between the soft sheets of the Savoy and Holmes' silky warmth. He lifted his upper body, resting on his fists, drew back and stroked in.

With a long, slow, hard rhythm, he thrust in and out of her, ensuring she felt each and every inch of his staff rubbing on her inner walls. He dragged himself back with determined precision before fucking back into her all the way to the base of his cock, then did it again. And again. And again. Rachel undulated her hips, wanting more and wanting it now.

Holmes responded by growling and getting to his feet, lifting her up and spreading her wide so she could do nothing but take what he wanted to give her in the way he wanted to give it. He pushed himself deep inside her, holding himself against her, before pulling back out. Her pussy pulsed in harmony to the throbbing of his cock.

"Please," she said, trying to hold back.

"Uh-uh, your orgasms belong to me."

He reached under her and slapped her ass with a considerable amount of sting. In response, Rachel went off like a rocket, her pussy clamping down and convulsing rhythmically all up and down his length.

"That's better," he crooned. She yowled in frustration.

Rachel had found that while she enjoyed every single orgasm she experienced at his hands, she wasn't truly satisfied until she felt him flood her with his cum while her pussy milked his cock for every last drop.

She watched him, looking down and watching as his cock pressed forward and pulled back, fucking her, fucking his woman, having her because she was his and it pleased him to do so—in the same way it pleased him to watch her climax.

Increasing the strength of his grip around her thighs, he began to move harder and faster, his hips slamming his cock deep inside her as his own breathing became more erratic and labored. He shifted position ever so slightly, so that his cock hit her sweet spot with each stroke as he pounded into her, grunting and groaning as he hammered against her.

His fucking became frenzied and primal, and she responded in kind, writhing under his furious onslaught until she felt her orgasm sweep over her, sending wildfire through her veins. With a final, ferocious thrust, he held himself against her and released a torrent of cum into her.

CHAPTER 21

As the witching hour approached, those who had been chosen to fight the Ripper gathered in Rachel and Holmes' room.

"Same formation as before?" asked Watson.

"It seemed to work. No need to change it."

"Roark and Holmes up front, us helpless females in the middle…" Male growls surrounded them. "And the other two testosterone-ladened Neanderthals behind us," quipped Sage, ignoring them.

Right before the clock chimed three in the morning, the sky over the Thames began to crackle with lightning and thunder.

"It's back," said Saoirse in a sing-song voice, making Sage and Rachel laugh.

Suddenly the lights flickered on and off like a demented two-year old was playing with a light switch. Felix opened the door and peeked out.

"The phenomenon is apparently localized to just outside your balcony and in your room."

Holmes turned and smiled at Saoirse. "It looks like we've pissed it off royally."

"Good," whispered Saoirse. "It's going to be easier to trick if it's trying to put on a display to frighten us, thinking it'll weaken you."

The room went completely black as the sky lit up with flash lightning. The lock on the balcony door unlatched and was blown open as a huge opaque blob entered the room.

"I told you, you miserable sod. You can't have her. You aren't welcome here. Get out."

Rachel grabbed the watch and pushed past Holmes. "See what I have?"

The shape let out a desperate scream as it advanced on her. Holmes grabbed her, shoving her back behind him.

"You stay where I put you, Rachel. You move again and put yourself in further danger with this asshole, and so help me God, I'll take my belt to your ass and you will never sit down again."

"I love you too, Holmes," she said. When had the Ripper had lost the power to terrify her? she wondered, and realized it was the moment Holmes had first made love to her. If that thing thought he could defeat them and their love, it was not only evil; it was stupid.

Next to her, Saoirse raised and opened a saltshaker, poured some in the palm of her hand, stepped forward, and blew the salt at the apparition. It screeched again and retreated. The gush of wind that accompanied its escape furled the heavy drapes like sails on a boat caught in a gale, slamming the door behind it. Outside, the lightning and thunder ceased, and the electricity in the room was restored.

An eerie silence fell over the suite, like the pall at a funeral service.

"Everyone all right?" asked Roark.

"Some of them might be at the moment, but that won't be the case for all of them by the time we get down to the SUV," growled Holmes. He turned around and looked at those behind him. "Felix, if you and Watson could put together a care package like you did last night, that would be great."

"Yes, indeed," said Saoirse. "And can we have more of those orange-cranberry scones? They were delicious."

"I hope you're going to deal with this one," he pointed at Saoirse, "as well as your fiancé," said Felix.

Holmes quirked his eyebrow up. "She's not mine to deal with."

"*She's* not anyone's to deal with," said Saoirse. "Do I have enough time to take a quick nap and freshen up in that gorgeous shower?"

"I'd say you have about two hours," said Roark. "One of us will come and get you."

"Maybe we should take two vehicles," said Sage.

"One will be large enough," replied Roark. "After all, only four of us are going."

Before she could respond, Roark tossed his wife over his shoulder and headed back to their room.

"I'll make sure Ms. Madigan gets to her room," offered Felix.

"I'll just bet you will," said Holmes with a laugh.

Once everyone had left, he turned back to Rachel. "Bedroom, naked now."

∽

He hadn't wanted to spank her. It was the very last thing in the world he'd wanted to do, but he knew she needed to know there was a surety and consistency to his discipline. What had she been thinking, taunting the apparition like that? Eventually, he'd punished her to the point of tears and then made savage love to her, which she had responded to in a manner he could never have imagined. In the end, they couldn't be parted even long enough to shower and get dressed.

When they met the others in the lobby, Holmes was only a little surprised to see Roark without Sage. Of course, the fact that there was a distinct handprint on Roark's cheek was proof that Sage hadn't been pleased about it. But Roark was right; she would be safer here at the hotel with Felix and Watson, and he rather imagined Sage was in no shape to take a long drive.

They loaded into the SUV and made the long trek back to Ireland. By the time they arrived, Rachel had persuaded Saoirse to come visit them and be involved in their wedding. Holmes had offered to set up one of the guest rooms at the house in Chelsea for her exclusive use, telling her she could have her own key and leave whatever she needed there.

Once back at the farmhouse, Roark stretched out on her couch, Holmes and Rachel took, at Saoirse's insistence, her room, and Saoirse used her loft. Exhausted from the lack of sleep and stress, they all spent the better part of the day in a sound sleep.

The standing stones were about an hour's walk, and Roark woke everyone at midnight. Once again they used the torches, adding a fourth one for Roark, and carried wood to the site. Saoirse went through the same ritual, lighting braziers and casting salt. The only difference was this time there was a gap between two braziers with no salt to secure it.

They didn't have long to wait by the bonfire before the Ripper started his show—flash and bolt lightning, thunder that sounded like huge base drums being beaten, and the wind whirling all around them.

"Perfect," said Saoirse. "Banshees like a good storm."

As the melee raged around them, a misshapen rectangle with a kind of lump at the top like a head made its appearance. It beelined for the opening in the salt. Saoirse was certain the apparition would only take the bait from Rachel. Holmes and Roark's job was to keep the thing at bay until the banshees answered her call.

If they failed to show, Saoirse was prepared to banish the spirit into the watch to be held prisoner until they could find a way to destroy it.

As the wind roared and swirled all through the standing stones, Saoirse raised her arms to the sky, her hands outstretched.

> For this one who dwells in between in this darkest hour,
> I call upon my ancestors with their sacred power,
> I stand alone and command the banshees to come to the fore,
> crying for justice for all who have died,
> And humbly beseech you to drag this spirit back to the dark realm forever more!

Holmes hadn't known what to expect, but the loud, keening wail was a sound he would never forget. It seemed to drown out the storm and surround them, invading all of their senses. The banshees rode out of the night sky on a chariot pulled by dragons—roaring and spewing fire. The three women driving them looked to be beautiful maidens as they rushed toward the apparition. Their screeching threatening to drive them all mad. Two of them held their hands up to the sky, beseeching some unknown power while the third bore down on the apparition with malicious intent.

Too late, the creature realized there was no way out. It whirled around, testing the strength of the trap Saoirse had laid. As they closed in, the faces of the fair maidens turned to hideous crones, with sunken, hollow eyes and withered skin. The apparition tried to flee, but the banshees pursued him with increased vigor, zeal and screeching.

As they overtook the Ripper, they snatched him up, latching onto him and binding him with chains that clanged and rang out in the night. Their cries turned to demonic cackling as they wheeled back toward the sky, the driver now cracking a whip made of lightning to urge the dragons on faster. The Ripper screamed in agony—and Rachel was pulled forward as if the tether would drag her along. Holmes reached out to grab her, unwilling to lose her. If she was going to hell, he was going with her.

One of the banshees turned to face them, her visage returning to that of a beautiful maiden before it raised a great broadsword, bringing it down on the tether. With a snap, Rachel was propelled back into Holmes, the blade forever severing Rachel's connection to the Ripper. Rachel slumped down, but Holmes was able to save her from a fall. Roark caught Saoirse, and they watched as the banshees galloped off into the night and vanished—the storm and the Ripper's cries fading into nothing.

"I don't suppose anyone brought graham crackers, chocolate and marshmallows, did they?" asked Rachel.

"That sounds disgusting," said Holmes.

"I have so much to teach you," she said, leaning against him.

∽

Two weeks later, things were settling into a normal routine. The pocket watch that had once belonged to the Ripper had vanished. Luckily, Eddy was able to erase any mention of the thing ever having existed. They ensured Saoirse had recovered before heading back to England. Holmes and Rachel moved out of the Savoy and into the house in Chelsea.

He'd been back at work for the past week, but each night he returned to their home, practically attacking Rachel in his eager haste to get inside her. He was like a smitten teenager and couldn't seem to get enough. Why had he ever agreed to let her invite their friends for dinner? As he parked the SUV, he got a text telling him their guests had arrived, which he was sure was code for, 'keep it in your pants until they leave.'

"Hello, sweetheart. Can you feed them all and get rid of them quickly?" he grumbled, pulling her into his arms and kissing her thoroughly.

Taking that as a cue that he didn't need to behave

either, Roark wrapped Sage in his arms and kissed her until she was breathless.

"You know," said Watson to Felix, "I'd tell them to get a room, but I'm afraid we'd be left to cook for ourselves. How come you and I can't find the perfect woman for us?"

"Speak for yourself, Watson. I've found mine. Perhaps you'd best look somewhere other than Ireland."

Watson laughed. "Message received. Besides, I'm not sure I'd want some woman who consorts with creatures of another realm. Can you even imagine that? How weird would it be to know what was on the other side of the veil." He shook his head. "No. Give me some nice quiet shop girl who wants to sit at my feet at Baker Street and treat me like a king."

"And why would she do that?"

"Because I'd treat her like my queen."

Interested in how Roark, Holmes and Felix came out of the pages of Sage's books? Read all about it in ADVANCE, available for free on all retailers.

Thank you for reading *Negotiation!* I've got some free bonus content for you! Sign up for my newsletter https://www.subscribepage.com/VIPlist22019. There is a special bonus scene, just for my subscribers. Signing up will also give you access to free books, plus let you hear about sales, exclusive previews and new releases first.

Turn the page for a First Look into Submission: Masters of the Savoy, available for preorder now and releasing on December 2, 2021

Masters of the Savoy

Advance
Negotiation
Submission
Contract
Bound

If you enjoyed this book I would love if you left a review, they make a huge difference for indie authors.

As always, my thanks to all of you for reading my books.

Take care of yourselves and each other.

FIRST LOOK

SUBMISSION: MASTERS OF THE SAVOY

May 1, 1536
Greenwich Palace
London, England

"My lady, the king loves you…"

"He does not. His fickle heart now belongs to Jane Seymour. The pasty-faced bitch can have him. I pray you to do this one last favor for me and watch over, as best you can, my daughter Elizabeth."

"But Queen Anne…"

"Have you not heard, Madge? I am no longer queen. Our marriage will be annulled as if it never happened, and Elizabeth will be declared bastard."

"The trial..."

"…is nothing more than playacting so they can write it in the history books that I was tried and convicted. Henry seeks to turn his people on me, so he doesn't garner their disdain when he puts me aside as he did with Catherine. Know that I did not do what they accuse me of, but it will not matter. I will die so that Henry can have the Seymour spawn. She is not strong enough to carry his sons, and like Catherine, any he manages to get on her will die."

"My lady, do not say such things…"

"Madge, please, one last favor?"

"Of course."

Anne pressed the small box, its edges sealed and then wrapped in oil cloth and sealed again, into her hands. "Take this and make your way to Wolsey's wine cellar. In the very back, there is a small cask of malmsey wine. There is an opening on the bottom. If you tip the cask forward, you can easily reach it and place the box in the wine barrel. Make sure no one sees you."

"Maybe you should try to run away?" suggested Madge.

"To where? I am the great whore of England, and the king wants me dead. So dead I shall be. Maybe I deserve it, not because I am guilty of that which I am accused, but because I coveted another woman's husband for power… and yes, for love. I was a fool. Never surrender yourself to the notion of love, Madge. It does not exist. Now hurry. God bless you, Madge, and remember me in your prayers."

She watched her lady-in-waiting run to do her bidding one last time and then sat down to wait for the end to come. There had been a time she loved

Henry and she thought he had loved her, but now she realized she had always been a pawn in a game of power in which she had no standing.

Anne sank to her knees and began to pray, not for her own soul, but for the Lord Jesus to watch over her daughter and keep her safe from the cruel machinations of men.

∽

May 19, 1536
Tower of London
London, England

She was to die this morning. She had watched from the window in her cell as her brother, George, was beheaded just two days before. Her only remaining ladies in waiting beseeched her not to watch, but she felt responsible for George's death. He had done nothing but serve Henry faithfully and love her as a brother should. And now he was dead. In just a little while, she would join him. But if it were possible, she would find a way to cling to the realm that lay between this one and eternal joy.

They came for her—tall, burly men with weapons. What did they think she was going to do? Overpower them with her wit and fly away? Fools, but she could not condemn them for they only did their master's bidding. Master. The word made her want to retch. She had taken great care with her last appearance before the small crowd that had gathered to watch her die. She wore a dark grey gown of the finest material and an ermine mantle. She covered her hair with a white linen coif for purity.

Slowly she walked toward her execution, but not her final fate if she had anything to do with it. She paid the executioner and then turned to address the crowd in what would be recorded as her last words—at least in this time and place—last only if she didn't find a way to hold on somewhere in the realm between heaven and hell.

"Good Christian people, I am come hither to die, for according to the law, and by the law I am judged to die, and therefore I will speak nothing against it. I am come hither to accuse no man, nor to speak anything of that, whereof I am accused and condemned to die, but I pray God save the king and send him long to reign over you, for a gentler nor a more merciful prince was there never: and to me he was ever a good, a gentle and sovereign lord. And if any person will meddle of my cause, I require them to judge the best. And thus I take my leave of the world and of you all, and I heartily desire you all to pray for me."

Anne knelt, repeating the simple prayer, "O Lord have mercy on me, to God I commend my soul."

When the executioner called for his sword, she looked toward where it might come from. She felt pain only for the flash of a moment as the blade's clean, sharp edge removed her head from her body in a single blow. As her ladies wailed in grief, Anne felt free for the first time in her life. If there was a chance for another, she would take it—patience and planning would be her guides. The pull to go to the light was strong, but she resisted, removing herself from its blinding path and returning to the dark tower.

One day, she promised herself, I will leave this place and live the life that was denied me. One day I will be free.

ABOUT THE AUTHOR

Other books by Delta James: https://www.deltajames.com/

If you're looking for paranormal or contemporary erotic romance, you've found your new favorite author!

Alpha heroes find real love with feisty heroines in Delta James' sinfully sultry romances. Welcome to a world where true love conquers all and good triumphs over evil! Delta's stories are filled with erotic encounters of romance and discipline.

∾

If you're on Facebook, please join my closed group, Delta's Wayward Pack! Don't miss out on the book discussions, giveaways, early teasers and hot men!

https://www.facebook.com/groups/348982795738444

ALSO BY DELTA JAMES

Masters of the Savoy
Advance - https://books2read.com/advance
Negotiation – https://books2read.com/negotiate
Submission - https://books2read.com/submission1
Contract – https://books2read.com/contract1
Bound – https://books2read.com/bound3

Fated Legacy
Touch of Fate - https://books2read.com/legacytof
Touch of Darkness - https://books2read.com/legacytod

Touch of Light – https://books2read.com/legacytol
Touch of Fire – https://books2read.com/legacyfire
Touch of Ice – https://books2read.com/legacytoi
Touch of Destiny – https://books2read.com/legacydestiny

Syndicate Masters
The Bargain - https://books2read.com/thebargain

Masters of the Deep
Silent Predator - https://books2read.com/silentpredator
Fierce Predator – https://books2read.com/Fiercepredator

Ghost Cat Canyon

Determined - https://books2read.com/ghostcatdetermined

Untamed - https://books2read.com/ghostcatuntamed

Bold - https://books2read.com/ghostcatbold

Fearless - https://books2read.com/ghostcatfearless

Strong - https://books2read.com/ghostcatstrong

Boxset - https://books2read.com/Ghostcatset

Tangled Vines

Corked – https://books2read.com/corked1

Uncorked - https://books2read.com/uncorked

Decanted - https://books2read.com/decanted

Breathe - https://books2read.com/breathe1

Full Bodied - https://books2read.com/fullbodied

Late Harvest - https://books2read.com/lateharvest

Boxset 1 – https://books2read.com/TVbox1

Boxset 2 – https://books2read.com/Tvbox2

Mulled Wine – https://books2read.com/mulledwine

Wild Mustang

Hampton - https://books2read.com/hamptonw

Mac - https://books2read.com/macw

Croft – https://books2read.com/newcroft-dj

Noah - https://books2read.com/newnoah-dj

Thom - https://books2read.com/newthom-dj

Reid - https://books2read.com/newreid-dj

Wayward Mates

Brought to Heel: https://books2read.com/u/m0w9P7

Marked and Mated: https://books2read.com/u/4DRNpO

Mastering His Mate: https://books2read.com/u/bxaYE6

Taking His Mate: https://books2read.com/u/4joarZ

Claimed and Mated: https://books2read.com/u/bPxorY

Claimed and Mastered: https://books2read.com/u/3LRvM0

Hunted and Claimed: https://books2read.com/u/bPQZ6d

Captured and Claimed: https://books2read.com/u/4A5Jk0

Printed in Great Britain
by Amazon